A LOST CHILDHOOD

By Santina M Clelland

Published 2008 by arima publishing

www.arimapublishing.com

ISBN 978 1 84549 297 7

Printed and bound in the United Kingdom

Typeset in Garamond 12/16

Swirl is an imprint of arima publishing.

arima publishing
ASK House, Northgate Avenue
Bury St Edmunds, Suffolk IP32 6BB
t: (+44) 01284 700321

www.arimapublishing.com

Dedicated to my mother for the benefit of her Grandchildren.

Chapter One

North Africa, a land of golden sand and sunshine: this is where I was born, in Tripoli, Libya.

My Sicilian parents emigrated here when Italy colonized the territory after Mussolini came to power.

My father was a member of the Sicilian Division of the Italian para-military police, the Carabinieri. He was part of the mountain section carrying out patrols on horseback. My mother became his bride by arrangement between their respective families, as was the accepted custom on the island

Both came from the province of Caltanisetta, living in a small town called Gela, near the sea. There was very little work available most of the men were employed on the fishing boats or on the land. Although my father was secure in his employment with the Carabinieri, they were not popular with the Sicilian population. This was due, no doubt, to their misplaced loyalties to or possibly their fear of the Mafia, who held great sway on the island.

When Mussolini offered the opportunity to emigrate to North Africa, with the promise of accommodation for families and the guarantee of employment, my parents saw this as their opportunity. They felt this would be the start of a new life for them and looked forward to bringing up a family in a land that seemed to offer the future prospects they so longed for.

The Italian government was encouraging young couples like my parents to make the move to North Africa. Security was assured for those families who decided to make the move to this new colony. Thus my parents made their decision and sailed from Sicily to Tripoli.

They were among the hundreds of young Italians sailing from Napoli, Genova and Sicily to start a new life in Africa. These were, in the main, young families who were to be the pioneers in this Italian Colony. They had left Italy with sorrow in their hearts as they were leaving behind their loved ones, relatives and friends and their country of birth. But they also came with an expectancy of a prosperous future for themselves and their offspring.

It was not easy and they had to endure many trials and tribulations. This was North Africa, there were no roads no proper means of transport and, above all very little water. However, these determined people persevered and with hard work they transformed the desert into a viable civilisation. From the sand grew beautiful cities and their ingenuity provided water and subsequently an abundance of vegetation.

Although my mother was ten years younger than my father this was not unusual at that particular time and they seemed very compatible. As they settled into their new life they decided it was time to start the family they both longed for. The first-born was my brother Marcello and eighteen months after, I was born.

We lived on the outskirts of the city on an estate of bungalows that had been built specifically for the workers from Italy. The community, therefore, was made up of families from diverse backgrounds. However, all were Italian, proud of their nationality and determined to make secure, prosperous lives for their families.

So it was we made lots of friends and other relatives joined us including, eventually, my paternal grandparents. Our bungalow was not very big consisting of three bedrooms, living room, kitchen, shower room and toilet.

As the family grew and my brother, Emanuele, and sister, Pina, were born bedrooms had to be shared. We were a close, happy family enjoying the beautiful sunny climate provided by North Africa. Perhaps we did complain, from time to time that it was too hot but this was little or no drawback to our happiness.

Life continued in a quiet leisurely fashion and my youngest sister Antonietta was eventually born. Marcello and I attended school while Emanuele and Pina were cared for at home.

However, our grandparents now joined us and our accommodation was, of course, cramped. Grandfather shared the boys' bedroom and grandmother that of the girls. By this time my father had purchased a lorry and built up a successful business transporting materials for those companies who were engaged in the many building projects commissioned in Tripoli.

The city of Tripoli had been gradually transformed from a small desert town to a rich, thriving port. Naturally, the port activity brought business to the town, which grew into an important city on the North African coastline. Further inland drilling for oil was taking place and this too added to the importance of the city's position.

The 2nd June 1940 was a day like any other. We went off to school and had quite an enjoyable day of lessons. Returning home at the usual time, Marcello and I found our parents sitting at the dining table talking to two police officers. I was apprehensive: what had happened, what was wrong? Staring anxiously at my parents faces I did not see any trace of worry there, their expressions were quite normal.

It transpired that the Italian government had offered to transport several hundred children to Italy for a three-month holiday. This was offered to all those Italian families who wished to take advantage. The government would pay all expenses. My sister Antonietta was too young to be able to benefit from this offer but the four of us were eligible. I hovered in the background listening and becoming quite excited at the prospect of going on holiday, especially to Italy.

I let my mind wander to this beautiful country I had heard so much about and the dream holiday that we would share. I was puzzled that the time scale mentioned was three months. This seemed a very long time for a holiday, especially when it was explained that our parents would not be coming with us. Nevertheless it sounded exciting, a voyage by ship. All we children could imagine was sand, sea, sunshine and the fun that we were going to experience.

We were, after all the children of those immigrants who had come here at the behest of the Italian Government to colonise this country on their behalf. It made sense that this same government were now able to offer an opportunity for the children to visit Italy to which they declared loyalty but which they had never even seen

The following few days were spent in preparation. Our clothes and favourite toys were packed ready for the long journey. In countless homes throughout the estate similar preparations were taking place although there were some families who decided against their children going. On the morning of our departure we assembled at the Town Hall where we were met by a number of officials. One teacher was allocated to each fifty children.

As I gazed up at the teacher allocated to our party I had a distinct sense of foreboding. She was a thin, angular woman of austere appearance. She wore thick spectacles through which she peered with an expression of cold disdain. We were transported to the port of Tripoli for embarkation. Four merchant ships were waiting to sail to Ravenna. There was an amazing 13,000 children to be transported to Italy and five ships had already left, bound for Naples.

Once on board we found the accommodation cramped and very basic. There seemed to be an endless number of camp beds, wherever you looked there were beds, very little room remained for us to move about. Although somewhat disillusioned, we tried to keep our flagging spirits up by thinking of Italy. However, the reality of the situation was beginning to dawn, where were we going? Who was really going to look after us? My younger brother and sister were only five years and three years old respectively and I realised they would rely on me a great deal. So how old was I ? I was all of seven and a half and my older brother, Marcello, was nearly nine years old.

The weather was perfect for a trip to sea; the sun was beating down from a clear blue sky. I looked around at the other children, they appeared to have no qualms, and excitement was everywhere as we assembled up on deck. Gazing down from the ship's rails we waved to our parents far below us on the quayside. The ship's engines then started and we began to sail slowly out of the harbour. The figures of our parents became smaller and smaller until they disappeared.

I then became aware of my feelings of trepidation. Here was I, a mere child of seven years having to take responsibility for my siblings, including my older brother. I was far more able than Marcello as he had been spoiled, being the eldest boy. So it naturally fell on my shoulders to fulfil the role of 'mother'. I pushed my anxieties to the back of my mind as I stared out across the calm blue sea.

I was imagining my mother as an eighteen-year-old bride making this same journey in the opposite direction. Thinking of her sailing to a new country, with a husband whom she hardly knew as the marriage had been arranged by their families. Somehow the thought of her and how she must have felt at that time, encouraged me, as my mother and father seemed to have grown close and appeared to have a happy life together.

Suddenly, I became aware of a group of sailors a little way away. They were talking among themselves and I strained to hear what they were saying. I heard one say, "Poor children, they are all so excited, anticipating their holiday, but they don't know there is going to be a war!" I pinched myself to make sure that I was not dreaming. Could what they were saying be true? Nobody had mentioned a war. Where were we going? What was our destination?

Another sailor agreed with the first. He added, "This will be no holiday, they could be away for years!" I was stunned, would we ever see our parents again? Tears came, then in a fit of rage and frustration I pulled off my shoes and threw them into the sea. I immediately regretted my impulse realising these were the only pair of shoes I possessed. I made my way down to our sleeping quarters where my younger brother and sister had already been put to bed and were fast asleep.

Suddenly I wanted my mother, wanted to feel her arms about me comforting and re-assuring me that all would be well. I felt very unhappy and vulnerable and threw myself on to the bed and cried myself to sleep. Waking suddenly, I found the teacher in charge standing over us. She looked very stern and did not exactly endear herself to us. When she spoke her words were clipped and her voice lacked any trace of warmth.

She told us we would have to behave ourselves and help one another during the long voyage as the teachers would be kept very busy preparing plans for our stay in Italy. When I told her that I had lost my shoes overboard she was very angry. She went away and then returned with a pair of shoes that I did not like very much. Trying them on, I told her that they were too tight; she told me that they were the only shoes available and I would have to wear them.

As time passed and we proceeded to our destination over a magnificent blue sea under a clear cloudless sky, I became aware of the lamentable noises coming from other parts of the ship. Children suffered from seasickness and often "threw-up" over themselves. Even, on occasion, over other nearby children when their stomach could no longer cope.

Taking time to look at other children, I realised that many of them were equally as unhappy and apprehensive as I was. Dirty, tear stained faces were everywhere. Children chattering in many different dialects made it sound worse. The sound of younger children who incessantly cried out "Mamma" was even more disturbing. Adults were significant by their absence and the children were left very much to their own devices.

This was not a passenger ship but an adapted cargo ship and the "human" cargo was being conveyed to an unknown fate. Arriving in Italy, the teachers were very much in evidence. However, they did not stand on ceremony but hurriedly marshalled us on to trains which were to take us inland. As our journey progressed we became aware of how different the landscape was from that of North Africa. This was a strange land to us, our homeland was Libya where our parents lived and where we had been born, although my mother always told us we belonged to Italy. At this moment in time I did not share her sentiments.

After a lengthy journey we arrived at the place that was to be our home for some time. A lot of confusion followed, as we were allocated dormitories. Our "home" was in Igea Marina, a very large building, part of a holiday complex by the sea which had been requisitioned by the government. There were several buildings which all looked the same which had been used for holidays by the sea for children from the cities, known in Italian as "Colonie Estive"

Each dormitory was now stark compared with what it must have looked like in the past. Sets of metal bunk beds and small bedside cabinets were now the only furnishings in each room. They stood uninvitingly whilst some thirty or forty children of various ages scrambled for a bunk. I made sure my younger sister and I had bunks together. What few belongings we had were brought to the room and each child was allocated a number.

Suddenly I realised that I had not seen my brothers since we boarded the train. Looking around the complex it soon became clear that only girls were here - no boys at all. I enquired of the teacher as to what had happened, what had gone wrong, where were my two brothers? The teachers could tell me nothing; they appeared completely uninterested.

I was in a panic, I felt responsible for my brothers. I was already letting my mother down. I made my way to the Head Teacher's office, which was situated in the large reception hall. I was determined to find out what was happening. All around was chaos and confusion, people scurrying back and forth. I decided the only way to gain attention was to make a scene. I began to cry and scream, shouting my brothers' names as loudly as I could. This did provoke a reaction.

The door to the office opened and an elegant lady wearing what appeared to be a uniform confronted me. A dark well tailored uniform that gave her an air of authority. The lady rebuked me saying I should be ashamed of myself carrying on like this when the teachers were all very busy settling everybody in. Asking the reason for my conduct she frowned angrily when I asked where my brothers were. She responded sharply saying, "This is a girls' school, there will be no boys here!"

I froze, "Please miss, can you tell me where my brothers have gone?" I asked. Again her response was cold and angry, "I really have no idea and I am too busy to worry about this nonsense, go away and behave yourself". I rushed back to the dormitory grabbing my little sister and hugging her closely. I could not believe that the plan was to split up the brothers and the sisters. Nobody had bothered to inform us and we were not even given the chance to say goodbye.

There was, after all, a war on and we might never see each other again. Pina started to cry, I was hugging her so tightly. I loosened my grip and started to sob. We were alone now we only had each other. All our belongings were stamped with the number we had been allocated on arrival this became the easiest means of identification, we were now numbers and our names seemed insignificant. Further degradation was to follow, our hair was shaved off and we were issued with uniforms.

Was this not the system used in prison? We had done nothing to deserve this treatment, why were they treating us like this? This "dream holiday" was turning into a nightmare! The haircuts and uniforms made us all look alike in our white tops with the letter "M" on the front. This was, of course, the initial of the Italian leader Mussolini. Imagine all these young girls, even the tiniest, dressed in the same uniform, A black skirt, white top, black sandals, white socks and even a black hat.

Chapter Two

Again I wondered. We were dressed like soldiers and being treated like soldiers. These ladies/supervisors where had they come from? they seemed to have been chosen because they had no attachments or sensitivity. They had the bearing and presence of prison warders. What we did not know, of course, that they had been specifically chosen for the task.

All were resident, they did not appear to have other homes or families. Each one was responsible for the supervision of all aspects of our well being, education, cleanliness. health care and what seemed the most important to them discipline. They controlled us with a "rod of iron" no allowances were made for age. Children from 4 to 15 all were expected to conform to the same strict rules

The strict regime did not allow for any deviation regardless of age or condition. We were awakened at an early hour each day and from then everything was according to the schedule. We were treated like "clockwork soldiers" from morning till night. This treatment caused a feeling of abandonment and insecurity. We had been abandoned by our family, there was absolutely no contact at all. There was no warmth or affection from the staff and the only visitors to the site were representatives of the Church and Government Officials. None of these visitors seemed sensitive to our needs.

The staff were referred to as our teachers. We soon learned that in order to avoid continual punishment we had to obey without question. It seemed to me that the most important task for these "teachers" was to turn us into creatures that would obey their every command. What was happening to us? This was supposed to be a holiday,

After a few days passed we were assembled together and addressed by the headmistress. She explained that we had been brought here because war had been declared. We had been evacuated for our own safety. We would enjoy a good life if we obeyed our teachers and this would be our home for the coming months.

We would eat, sleep and attend school on the premises. I could not envisage this, there appeared to be hundreds of children with very few adults to take care of us. I kept glancing across toward my group's teacher, Miss Palma. She would be our surrogate mother but I could not warm to her at all. My instinct told me she could be cruel and sadistic.

The days that followed were chaotic. Disorientated children who were like fish out of water. They were unable to take in or understand the magnitude of the situation. They felt very much abandoned by their parents and dearest relatives. We would often stare at each other not sure whether to make friends or keep our distance but then the sight of each other's bald heads would often make us feel like giggling. So many varying shapes and sizes, all with shaven heads and dressed in the same uniform must have been quite a spectacle.

Each one of us went through the process of being measured, weighed and registered. And now our clothing and other personal items were taken away. We were left with nothing to connect us to our families and friends, we now only had our memories and some were too young even for those. We attended school where a rigid timetable was strictly observed. "Playtime" was also a very controlled part of our day. We were taught fascist songs along with the history of Mussolini and how he only had our interests at heart. We must not let him down. Our motto was "Believe, obey and fight", this was what "Il Duce" wanted from us, our country needed us.

The school added to this motto "Order and Discipline" and there was no forbearance for those who did not follow the rules. Each teacher had sworn to teach us, using whatever methods were necessary, to indoctrinate us in the cause of Mussolini. Any child who did not comply was placed on report and punishment invariably followed. We marched everywhere and were often ordered to shout "Viva IL Duce" "Viva Italia" "Viva i Fascisti" "Viva Hitler". We were made to do things in an almost robotic way without feelings. Gymnastics that I had always adored, I now loathed.

Somehow it felt as though a prison had been built around us. Even the simplest tasks became a rigid routine. Our enjoyment of life was curtailed and we were not free to use our imagination. I used to look at the birds and wish I could change places with them, fly away, take my sister and brothers with me back to our beloved home and family. We began to recognise the sound of the air raid sirens and could hear planes above us when we made our way to the cellars. Somehow it all seemed unreal, as we had seen no signs of the war. One night I awoke suddenly, startled from a deep sleep. Sitting up in my bunk, I looked around. I was alone in the room; there were no other children there. Looking for my sister, I panicked; she was not there either. A dim light shone in the corridor, all the windows were covered by heavy black blinds. There was no sound from any of the other rooms. Eerie silence threatened to overwhelm me. Where had everyone gone? Why was I the only person left in this huge silent building? I ran anxiously down the corridor searching desperately for someone - anyone. Suddenly I heard the sound of approaching aircraft followed by explosions. I crouched in a corner and screamed in terror. No one heard me. I felt as though I was the only person left on earth. My body was frozen with fear, was this the last moment of my life? Would I ever see anyone again? These thoughts ran rapidly through my mind. I did not want to be so alone, please God, help me! I continued to sit there in a state of terror only aware of my own sense of fear and isolation.

After what seemed hours the all-clear siren sounded and I became aware of voices. The other children were returning to their rooms from the cellars far below. I realised that I must have slept through the warning siren. I had not slept very well for several nights I pushed these thoughts to the back of my mind as my little sister returned with the other children, she was still half asleep, we hugged and I thanked God that she was safe. I tucked her up in her bed and she immediately fell asleep. I began to fret at the thought of my two brothers, did they have each other? I did not know I began to wonder if we would ever see them again. I climbed back into my bunk feeling desperately lonely, I longed for my mother and cursed the dream holiday that was now a nightmare and softly cried myself to sleep.

Chapter Three

One day during our break outside I became aware of how beautiful the sea was and with the glorious blue sky and sunshine I could almost allow myself the luxury of smiling. My little sister had become my shadow, wherever I was she was there holding my hand, afraid to let go. I also had become obsessed and afraid of losing her. From my family of nine, including Grandma and Granddad, I now only had my little sister left with me.

I had tried to make friends with other girls and even Miss Palma but I was so wrapped up in my innermost feelings that I just could not. On this beautiful day I saw two vans delivering vegetables. I looked longingly at the vegetables. The food we were served was meagre and unappetising; we were all hungry. By reaching through the bars of the gate, I found it possible to touch the carrots. I drew one through and gave it to Pina. Then I stretched again and took another two or three carrots. There seemed nothing wrong with these actions, especially as Pina and I were hungry. Another two or three girls followed my lead and they also took carrots.

We munched happily on the sweet roots, enjoying our unexpected treat. When later we went into dinner we said grace in the normal manner. Miss Palma then announced that girls had been seen stealing food. This was a crime worthy of the most severe punishment and, for the benefit of all, she asked that those responsible own up. In order to survive in this strict regime we had an unspoken code of unity. No one spoke, although we all knew the identity of the culprits. Was this honour among thieves?

Miss Palma became very angry and told us we would remain standing all through our dinner. This did not seem too dreadful a punishment. However, I was feeling nauseous. I had already been sick after eating the carrots so hurriedly. As I stood at the table I felt I was going to be sick again clasping my hand to my mouth I ran to the bathroom. When I returned to the table Miss Palma, furious with me for leaving the room, told me to eat my meal. My plea that, as I had just been sick and and was unable to eat anything fell on deaf ears.

Forced to eat, I took one or two mouthfuls of food but again I was overcome by nausea and had to rush from the dining room. Miss Palma was becoming more and more angry with me. She followed me into the bathroom, ordering me to return to the dining room immediately. During her brief absence the other children, thinking they were helping me, scraped what remained on their plates on to mine.

Their thinking was, Miss Palma could not possibly make me eat what was now on my plate. How wrong they were. My initial instincts about this woman had been right. She peered at me through her spectacles, her expression cold and hard. The message was clear, "How dare you defy me!" She told me I had to eat everything on my plate. Knowing she would show no mercy, I lifted the spoon and forced the food into my mouth. After only two mouthfuls I was retching violently. Her expression was one of triumph, I ate another couple of mouthfuls and then vomited. I felt dreadful and thought that at last I would be excused. I should have known better: this "teacher" forced me to eat everything on the plate including my own vomit! I now felt real hatred for this person, how could anyone accept her as replacement for a mother. The children from the other dormitories were allowed to go outside at break time, but the girls from my dormitory were marched upstairs. My younger sister who was only three years old was also subjected to this punishment as she belonged to the same dormitory. When we arrived upstairs we expected to be sent to bed as further punishment. This, to me, would have been welcome, I felt so ill.

However, this was not to be, Miss Palma had other ideas. She insisted that we knelt in the corridor outside her bedroom. Having done this she made us place our hands under our knees and told us we were to remain in this position until the culprits who had stolen the food owned up. Despite how uncomfortable we were, at that moment in time, we had no intention of owning up to anything. We thought she would only keep us there for a little while, maybe half an hour or an hour at the most.

We had no idea the extent of her cruelty. Miss Palma went to her room, telling us that under no circumstances were we to move. After about ten minutes our hands became very sore through lack of circulation, we were frightened and worried about the possible consequences should we move. We were all depressed yet there was a unity between us and we were determined we would not give in. We had only helped ourselves to a few carrots that after all had been delivered for our consumption.

The girls whispered to each other, telling stories. So engrossed were they in the storytelling nobody noticed that the door to Miss Palma's room was slowly opening. When she heard the whispering and saw that we were all sitting on the floor, her face contorted in fury. She seized a leather belt from her room and commenced striking us. We were all in tears; some of the girls were beaten more than others, as she frantically lashed out in her anger.

Was our crime so terrible that we deserved such cruelty? Once again Miss Palma ordered us back on our knees with our hands underneath them. Our pleading went unheard; we were left there for hours. The teacher would creep out of her room from time to time and again lash at us with the belt if any one had dared to move. By the early hours of the morning I was feeling desperately ill, I wanted to be sick and needed to use the toilet.

Each time Miss Palma came out of her room I asked permission to use the bathroom but my request was coldly denied. In the end there was no alternative, I was in such agony that I relieved myself where I knelt. When Miss Palma next came out of her room and realised what I had done she was again furious. She grabbed my head and wiped my face over the wet floor. After this incident she must have felt she had completely triumphed, we were given permission to go to bed.

I rushed to the bathroom and scrubbed myself clean with a scrubbing brush used to clean the floors. I was sobbing uncontrollably and could not understand why we were being subjected to such cruelty. My parents had always been good to us, gentle and kind, I had never experienced this kind of violence before. Having been entrusted to the Government to protect us from the dangers of war, why were we now being subjected to such cruelty?

We should have taken our chances in Tripoli, we would, at least, have had loving, caring people around us to comfort and protect us in time of danger. It was bad enough that we were alone here with no one to hug us and make us feel secure, but to be abused like this was more than any child could bear. I curled up in my bunk feeling completely isolated, unloved and abandoned. Once again I cried myself to sleep, Our "carers" were such strict disciplinarians and so devoid of feelings we named them "Vigilantes"

Chapter Four

Teresa, a child who suffered with asthma, was occasionally left behind when we were marching or parading, due to her shortness of breath. During these times she used to explore the grounds and made friends with a stray dog. This dog somehow knew when Teresa would be alone and not under the scrutiny of the "vigilantes". They paid little attention to her, as they were too busy to worry about her.

One day Teresa. following her stray dog, in the surrounding grounds heard a cough coming from one of the empty sheds. She was curious, so she decided to investigate. The dog, she had named him Pippo, began to scratch at the door and Teresa called out "Is anyone there?" Silence followed, the dog began to bark and would not be quiet and poor Teresa was beginning to panic.

Relaying the story to us later. She said she thought that it might be a German soldier and, like me, she was very afraid of them. Slowly the door began to open, she could only see a hand, and it was very large. Teresa was beginning to breathe very hard and the threat of an asthmatic attack was very real. A voice hissed "Are you alone?" and Teresa realised he had a local accent and she relaxed a little. She said she was and asked the man what he was doing there. He said his name was Pietro. He was a partisan who was against fascism.

He had come down from the hills during the night looking for German soldiers. He had a narrow escape and had to hide away. He had run across the nearby wasteland into the grounds of the complex where he hid in the shed. His partisan friends had returned to the hills and he was hoping to meet up with them again at nightfall. He asked Teresa not to tell anyone he was there for his life would be in danger. Feeling both excited and afraid, Teresa had to tell someone. She confided in me on her return and I offered to save some food, which she could take to him.

I did not go with her, as she was afraid that Pietro would be angry if she brought someone else. The following day Pietro was gone and Teresa never saw him again. A week later Teresa was very upset, as she had found her stray dog dead. She could not come to terms with this as she had become very attached to Pippo. How could someone have been so cruel? They had killed the dog by cutting its throat.

Teresa suspected it might be the caretaker who had recently started working in the grounds of the school. He appeared a simple man who seemed very nervous and introvert. We felt he was always spying on us, as he would suddenly appear from nowhere. His smile displayed a mouthful of rotten teeth and his movements were sudden and jerky; his whole manner made us afraid of him.

We thought it strange that such a man was allowed to work here, a place completely run by females and almost five hundred small girls living on the premises. Teresa started to watch him and somehow he must have taken this to mean she was attracted to him. One night, after we had finished our marching, I was aware that Teresa, who had been on her usual time out, had failed to come to bed I began to worry about her and whispered to some of the other girls to be on the look out for her.

We could not let the "vigilantes" know, as she would be in a great deal of trouble if they knew she had been missing. Several trips were made, supposedly to the bathroom, but deviated to various windows of the building. We hoped we might spot her in the grounds. In order to ensure the "vigilantes" would not know she was missing we put a couple of pillows under her blankets so that it appeared she was in bed.

Then one of the girls ran into the dormitory saying that she had seen Teresa being dragged into the shed by the man who worked in the grounds. We were in a state of panic but were too afraid to let Miss Palma know. She would have been furious that we had not told her Teresa was missing. It was, therefore, up to us to rescue Teresa. To do this we had to get out through one of the large doors situated at the end of the corridor. The bolts were very high and one girl stood on another's shoulders to reach them. Managing to open the doors, we crept into the grounds and made for the shed.

As we approached we could hear Teresa crying. I shouted out to her, she stopped crying and called my name shouting, "Please help me". I frantically kicked at the door shouting, "Let her go you wicked man", I was not sure why I said that but my instincts told me that he had not dragged Teresa into the shed for nothing. In my innocence I had no idea what he could do to her, but I felt that whatever it was, it would not be good. The door remained locked and Teresa began to cry again shouting, "Don't touch me, get away from me!" Some of the girls ran back to the building. We now had no choice but to inform Miss Palma. Our hope was she would be able to stop whatever was happening to Teresa. Furious, she accompanied us to the shed where she banged on the door and commanded that it be opened immediately. I went to the window to see if I could see inside, I was horrified when I saw this man lying on top of Teresa, whose hands were tied above her head. The man's trousers were round his ankles. He got up when he heard Miss Palma's voice and, pulling his trousers round his waist, went to the door.

Miss Palma pushed past him followed by a girl called Maria and myself. Untying Teresa's hands she pulled her to her feet then shouted, "This is what happens when you disobey, you should not have been outside the building at this time. Maria and I tried to comfort Teresa who was about to have an asthma attack. She was grateful that we had saved her from what I later learned would have been rape.

Teresa became an even greater friend. The "caretaker" was never seen again and we never knew what action, if any, was taken against him. Teresa became very sad after this experience. She did not venture into the grounds alone again. The one and only time I saw anything like compassion from the "vigilantes" was on this occasion. Discovering she had an older sister, resident in another school they made arrangements for her to be transferred. Thus the sisters were reunited.

Chapter Five

During the periods of "playtime" when we had a break from lessons, marching and parading, we were allowed to wander in the grounds. However, there was little playing. Most of the children stood around and there was little or no interaction. Always there were at least two of the "vigilantes" keeping an eye on us.

When it was raining we were not allowed outside. On these occasions I passed my time looking out of the window. Holding Pina's hand we talked about our family wondering if everybody had forgotten us. I would imagine our mother with our youngest sister, who was by now at least six months old. I could see her with the baby, cuddling her close, singing to her.

I would then see tears in her eyes. She had lost four of her five children; I knew she would be pining for us as we were for her. I wondered, too, if my brothers ever thought of us. I thought of them often, wondering how they were, where they were.

Very occasionally we were taken in small groups to the town where we would walk through parks and gardens. This was the only time we saw other children, we envied their happy smiling faces and their smart clothing. They, in turn, looked at us strangely, I don't know what they thought of us.

On other odd occasions we were allowed to go to the woods, supervised of course. This was the only time I remember being happy. We took baskets with us and collected wild flowers and berries. I would lose myself in a fantasy world. Dreaming of our garden at home the vegetables and grapes we grew and the animals we kept in the garden.

After a few more months had passed, each monotonous day the same as the other, I became aware that one of the teachers was different from the rest. She seemed to have some compassion towards the children in her care. When we were outside she always had a smile and a gentle touch for whichever girl was standing near her, She was older than the other teachers and because of her seeming compassion we named her "Mamma Sarina".

The other "vigilantes" did not like her because they felt she was not strict enough with the children. One-day rumours went round that "Mamma Sarina" had been suspended from her job. These rumours turned out to be too true. The "vigilantes" said she was not capable of maintaining order. Her ways were not suitable. She did not believe in severe punishment, was too charitable and maternal.

There was no room for this kind of sentiment in a place like this. "Mamma Sarina" left our establishment. The morning she left she was wearing civilian clothes, carrying a suitcase. As she went through the gate we were not allowed to say goodbye. Many of us, however, shed tears and silently said our goodbyes. She turned as she went through the gate, gave us a long sad look and finally waved. We had lost the only sympathetic person who had appeared in this vile place. Once again, someone who might have made a difference to our life was taken away.

It was made clear to us that we were there to be regimented and disciplined; there was no room, apparently, for sentiment in this regime. After all we were there to learn, obey and, if necessary, fight for "Il Duce". The very next day, "Mamma Sarina's" replacement arrived. She was, like the others a veritable "vigilante"; she would keep us in order! She walked around with a stick, like an army sergeant -major. She made it clear she was "in command" and would tolerate no nonsense. We christened her "Marescialla"

I do not recall any good memories from this period. For all of us it was a time of sadness and despair. Most afternoons I gazed longingly at the entrance gate. I did not pay attention to any lessons. I visualised the day when my mother or brothers would come through that l gate and take Pina and myself away from this terrible place. I wondered how my brothers were coping, especially Emanuele, he was only five years old. Not knowing where they were or even if they were alive or dead made it even more agonising

What was I waiting for? I had no idea, but I felt such a sense of isolation. We had been a large family, a happy one. Now there was just Pina and I and strangers surrounded us. We had been told there was a war on. We had seen some signs of this but on the whole life seemed better out there. What did this war have to do with us? Why had there been the need to separate 13,000 children from their families and homeland? For what purpose were we being trained?

As a nine year old child I was asking a lot of questions but not getting any answers.

One of the older girls told me that when she was unhappy or wanted something very badly she would say a special prayer her mother had taught her. I asked if she would teach me this prayer. She agreed and I learned it quickly. She told me if I repeated this prayer every night for thirty days whatever it was I wished for would come true.

Chapter Six

What I prayed for did not materialise but things did change. One morning after breakfast some of us were gathered together and told to pack what meagre belongings we had. No explanation was given and there seemed no specific reason for those selected, it appeared simply random. We were fortunate that Pina and I were both selected as any parting would have been devastating.

Loaded on to coaches we had no idea where we were going. We hoped we were being returned home but this was not to be. The coaches seemed to travel for ever but it must have been only a couple of hours before we arrived at our destination. It is difficult to describe our feelings, curiosity of course, but any excitement was dampened by our anxiety.

Scrambling out of the coaches we were marshalled together in lines like soldiers. However, as we stood there I was impressed by the enormous building before us. It was resplendent with huge windows and balconies. Sweeping marble steps led up to an enormous entrance. Two very large doors stood open before us and we could see the opulence of the interior. To either side of the steps were magnificent Palm trees and we were surrounded by gardens.

This was so very different from the stark surroundings we had left. Why were we here? We later learned that this building (which was in fact a first class hotel in this Northern Province of Italy which had in the past been frequented by the rich tourists from the rest of Europe) had been sequestrated by the Authorities. We had been moved further North because of the invasion by the Allied forces further South.

We were ordered into the building where we discovered the interior was as impressive as the outside. Marble floors and a huge mahogany desk greeted us but the outstanding feature was the huge marble staircase leading to the first floor. Whilst we were in awe of our surroundings our curiosity was now at its height. We couldn't wait to see what else lay before us.

We were herded up the beautiful staircase into corridors equally elegant as the floor below. I then realized that furniture, curtains and decorations were noticeable by their absence. Despite the opulence of the building its interior was quite bare. We were being allocated sleeping quarters, so I held on tightly to Pina's hand making sure we were not separated.

Eventually we were told to enter a room, where we were faced with the reality of our situation. Gone were the luxurious furnishings of this large room and to replace them were eight metal beds each with a small locker. However, this was much better than our previous accommodation, only half the number of children to a room and certainly more space. The other six girls were all known to us so we were happy to be settled in this our room which was recognizable by the number on the door.

Although the staff who had accompanied us were the same "Vigilantes" they had a lot of administrative work to do now so after being allocated our rooms we were at liberty to explore our surroundings outside. Our first impression had not been wrong, this was a very large building, The imposing main structure in the centre was flanked on each side by more practical structures consisting of two floors with smaller windows to the rooms.

The whole edifice was surrounded by beautiful gardens with several exotic plants, shrubs and palm trees. The grounds were enclosed within a stone wall interspersed with wrought iron railings. A wide drive swept in a beautiful curve to the huge ornate gates. We could not believe our luck, to be in such magnificent surroundings after our previous barrack like accommodation. It was sheer bliss to walk through the gardens with the scent and beautiful colours of the flowers.

Things were about to return to what we had come to accept as normal, however, as only the surroundings had changed for the better. Our "Vigilantes" were still our keepers and the regime resumed as in our previous situation.

As it was now two years since we had last seen our parents I decided I would concentrate solely on the prayer and my wish, to see my mother and be re-united with her. I could hardly wait for bedtime so that I could say my prayer time and time again, "Oh God, please make my wish come true". After a few days of constant praying I felt a sense of peace. I believed in this prayer whole-heartedly and taught my little sister to say it with me.

Two weeks went by and then the headmistress called Pina and me to her office. She handed me a letter, which had come from our mother. I couldn't believe my eyes. The letter contained a photograph of our youngest sister Antonietta who was now two years old. I did not recognise her, she was only a month old when we left.

The letter read: My darling children, I have been searching desperately for you. I have written everywhere to try and find you. I never dreamed, when we agreed to let you go for a holiday, that we would not see you for a long time, or that we would not be informed of your whereabouts. I am so sorry and have regretted our decision to let you go.

I will do my utmost to get you home and re-unite the whole family. I still do not know where your brothers, Emanuele and Marcello are but I am frantically trying to trace them. Every official avenue that is open to me I will pursue. Father, Grandma and Granddad are all well. Your father is as desperate as I am to get you all back home together.

The war is quite fierce in these parts but I have found the Captain of a boat who is willing to give me passage to Italy. It will cost a lot of money, but at the moment the only matter of importance is to get you all back home. Lots of love from all of us and I hope to see you very soon and give you lots and lots of kisses. You are always in my thoughts Love Mamma.

We read the letter over and over again. We cried with joy and thanked God that he was already granting us part of the wish we were praying so hard for. The letter brought such happiness that I kept pinching myself, to make sure I wasn't dreaming. I knew my mother would come. Would she recognise us? Would we recognise her?

Each day I stood watching longingly through the bars of the front gate. Would our mother come today? Then came the thirtieth day of my prayers, this day my prayer should be answered! I would soon know if God listens to children. A girl approached me and told me the Head wanted my sister and I to go to her office. The girl went on to say that our mother was here. Not believing her, I was angry that she should tease me in this manner. "It's true," she insisted, "Your mother is here with your baby sister."

I grabbed Pina by the hand and we ran as fast as we could into the entrance hall. There, the headmistress was waiting for us, she was actually smiling. She took our hands and led us into her office. I had never seen her in this light before. Entering, I could not believe my eyes, I immediately recognised my mother. I ran into her outstretched arms, we embraced, kissed, laughed and cried. A feeling of pure joy engulfed me; surely this must be the happiest day of my life. I refused to release my hold on my mother afraid that if I did she would disappear.

In my excitement I had not anticipated that Pina would not recognise our mother. She had forgotten her and was very reluctant to show the same enthusiasm as me. Only three years old when we left home in the subsequent two years that had passed she had come to look on me as a mother figure. I did all the things that a mother would normally do such as kissing, hugging her, and tucking her up in bed at night

Pina was a very good child. She seldom cried and would place her hand, trustingly, in mine and follow me wherever I went. She was my constant shadow. All this time, however, my heart was crying out that I, too, was only a child - that I needed a mother's love also. Now our mother was here at last, she would be able to resume her proper role and I could attempt to pick up on my own childhood.

Mother was allowed to take us out for the rest of the day. She was going to see an apartment to let and it was her intention to live there in order to be near us. This was a blow to us as we had hoped to resume our life together as a family. She explained she was not yet in a position to take us out of the school because she was very short of money, and due to the war our father was unable to send any money to Italy. Although this is not what we had expected, at least we had our mother close to us again.

Mother told us she was still desperately trying to trace our brothers. This she could not do if she had the responsibility of looking after three children. I asked her to promise us that she would never let us go as before but would be there to see us as often as she could. This she promised. I made a fuss of my sister Antonietta, she was a gorgeous baby.

Pina was beginning to have confidence with mother and was obviously enjoying her deep affection.

We returned to the school but life took on a new meaning from then on. Even the "vigilantes" seemed less austere than before. Perhaps this was because our mother was a regular visitor to the school. A few days later mother informed us that she had received a letter from a government official. This gave her the address of our brother's school, mother would have to leave for a short while to go and find them. I cannot describe the sense of fear that filled my heart. Would we ever see mother again?

I had to remind myself that, as she had found us, so she must go and find our brothers but I was terrified of losing her again. However, I had to accept the situation and clung to the hope that very soon we would all be reunited. The thought of seeing my brothers again filled me with joy. Each day mother was away I grew more and more anxious. Finally, after ten days, she returned with my brothers, Marcello and Emanuele. I hardly recognised them. They too had had their heads shaved and were wearing uniforms. They resembled miniature soldiers. Marcello had recognised mother but Emanuele had the same problem as Pina. He had been only five years old when we left home. I could tell from their expressions and their sunken eyes that they had also suffered in the last two years. However, we were overjoyed to be back together again. Several weeks later mother discharged us from the school. The "school" that was more like an army training camp. I was certainly not sorry to leave the place but I did feel sorry for the girls we had left behind. They would continue to suffer under the cruel "Vigilantes".

Chapter Seven

We attempted to establish some kind of family life but we had very little money. Mother visited various official departments begging for help. She wanted to keep us together and, hopefully, get us back to Tripoli. The answer was always the same, "Sorry, there is nothing we can do, there is a war on!"

We tried to economise in every way we could. Marcello went fishing as often as possible, hoping to catch something from which we could make a meal. Any kind of fish would do, just so long as it was safe to eat. I took Pina into the woods where we collected edible berries and wild vegetables. Mother sold what little jewellery she had, in order to keep us together. With five children to feed and the money father had given her before she left Tripoli already all gone, her despair was apparent. She desperately tried to get work but these were not normal times.

One day she called us together and gave us some terrible news. We would have to go into children's homes, there was no choice. This was devastating to us all. After what we had been through during the last few years, we did not relish the idea of going through it again. Mother did promise, however, she would try to find better places than the establishments where we had been so unhappy.

We journeyed some miles before reaching a convent where it was agreed Pina and I could be accommodated. The sisters, however, would not take our brothers and once more we were forced to be apart. Mother did find another convent some ten miles away where our brothers could be accommodated. She also managed to find cheap lodgings situated a convenient distance from both convents. She would be able to visit us all fairly regularly. Antonietta was too young to be accommodated in the convent so she stayed with mother.

My memories of the convent are good even though the regime was both strict and religious, the nuns were very kind. We were woken each morning at 6 a.m., washed, dressed and went to the chapel before breakfast. Attendance at chapel was, obviously, a necessary part of the regime. I did not have any objections to this as I was at peace with God since my mother's appearance in answer to my prayer. I still said prayers every night to show my gratitude to Him. As I attended the chapel regularly I seemed to enjoy a kind of inner peace.

The fact that we had been re-united with my brothers and youngest sister, too, went a long way towards my feelings of contentment. After breakfast we attended school. As I was one of the older girls in the convent I enjoyed certain privileges. My sister and I shared a bedroom on the top floor, it was only an attic room but it was wonderful to have such privacy.

In the evenings when Pina had fallen asleep, I would lose myself in a fantasy world. I dreamt of someday returning to our beloved country and being all together as a family. Perhaps I would become a famous dancer. I imagined myself in beautiful dresses, dancing on stage in front of a large audience. At the end of my performance there was a wonderful response everyone standing, applauding until their hands were sore.

Time passed quickly here, a year had soon passed. Mother did visit us regularly but as we did not leave the convent, we did not see my brothers and depended on mother passing on their news. The boys, too, seemed much happier in the convent but I sometimes wondered if we were ever going to live all together with our mother again.

The war seemed much closer here. We could hear the bomb blasts and occasionally heard news that someone close by had either lost his or her life or home. The nuns protected us from the outside world. We were only really afraid when we were suddenly woken in the night and had to run to the air raid shelter. This was underground, at the bottom of the convent garden. It was quite terrifying, running through the dark when suddenly the sky would be lit up by a bomb exploding. The noise was frightening and it was almost like it was daylight.

The nuns tried to comfort us in the shelter and encouraged us to pray. Sometimes we would sing to keep our spirits up. The songs, of course, were not those we had been taught in our former school. At these times I would start to worry about my mother, sister and brothers and panic would fill my heart. I felt safe in the convent, so much so, that sometimes I would not look out of the windows for days on end. This was so unlike the two years spent at the other school, when I would gaze out of the windows endlessly, longingly.

As time passed, however, I became more curious about the outside world. I was growing older and it was almost as if I'd woken from a dream. I started to look from my attic window quite regularly. One day I heard quite a commotion from outside so I opened the shutters wide and peered down. There appeared to be many people standing around in the street.

They were strangely silent and some even seemed to be weeping. Lorries with German soldiers came down the street. Some were open topped and I saw in one several young women, completely naked and with their heads shaven. These women hung their heads and tried to cover their nakedness with their hands and arms, crouching as low as they could get.

The German soldiers seemed oblivious to the quiet sobbing and obvious unhappiness of the onlookers. They were laughing and joking among themselves. The convoy passed. I felt a sickening feeling in the pit of my stomach. I hurriedly closed the window; I felt that I never ever wanted to open it again. What was happening to the world outside? I rushed down to seek out the sisters and tell them of what I had seen. Who were these people, were they Jews or Italian girls who had betrayed the Germans. Where they on their way to a concentration camp? Whoever they were, the German were making example of them. What I saw in their faces will live in my memory forever.

Chapter Eight

After another eighteen months at the convent, our mother decided she wanted us to be living as a family again. Without us she had been able to obtain work, and had managed to save a little money. She had also been successful in obtaining an allowance from the government, which, although small, made her feel she would be able to care for us again. Despite all the setbacks and difficulties, my mother only wanted us to be together.

Mother had found a small apartment she was able to rent. The apartment was very cramped for the six of us, but this was a small sacrifice to make in order that we could be together as a family. I helped with the cooking, cleaning and washing to enable mother to carry on working. We were enrolled into new schools. Marcello was now attending senior school. Mother, realising that I desperately wanted to learn to dance, even achieved this. She enrolled me for dancing classes.

At last we were all so happy. The time came for the end of year party at Marcello's school and we were invited to attend. I was slowly maturing and becoming conscious of my appearance. I desperately wanted a new dress for the party. Mother came up trumps again, managing to scrape together enough money to buy material, a beautiful sky blue colour with a small white star pattern. She had done very little sewing in the past but sat up all night in order to make my dress.

The dress was everything I could have wished for but I did not possess any shoes to wear. We all wore wooden clogs; they lasted much longer than shoes. I must have looked a sight in these but I didn't care, I was happy. As it was winter, snow fell often in the north of Italy and our wooden clogs provided little protection, and chilblains were not uncommon. Although my feet were red and swollen, I paid little heed to my discomfort as I danced to the wonderful music. The end of year party is one of the happiest memories I have of that time in my life.

During the next six months life passed fairly quietly. We struggled on, finding it hard to make ends meet sometimes but happy that we were together and being cared for by our dear mother. I continued to attend dancing classes and made friends with a girl called Lucia. She was also twelve years old, though but much different from me in colouring and stature, she was blonde and delicate. We discovered we lived only a few doors from each other, which gave us the opportunity to see each other out of class.

Lucia lived with her mother and brother. Paulo, who was eighteen. Her father had recently been killed while serving at the front in the forces and her older brother of twenty-six was also in the army. I introduced Lucia to my mother and shortly afterwards our parents met, became good friends and spent a great deal of time together. They were able to support and comfort each other as they both missed their husbands.

I grew particularly fond of Lucia and we became quite inseparable. I also had a crush on her brother Paulo. We were now becoming very much aware that the war was having a terrible effect on the people around us. There were rumours that several German soldiers had been found dead. It was alleged Italians had killed them. This confused me, were they not our allies? Why would we kill them? Nothing seemed to make sense any more. People were dying, families were devastated. At least we were all alive and, despite our discomfort and unhappiness in the past, we were able to continue with our lives.

Then came the day our dancing teacher informed us we had been chosen to perform a series of dances at the local Opera House. We all worked very hard having rehearsals every night. Then we rehearsed on stage, alongside adult dancers and singers. I was enchanted by it all and being at an impressionable age, decided that I wanted to become a dancer more than anything else. I gave up every spare minute to rehearse, which helped in my attempt to blot out the last few years.

We were to appear, as part of the chorus, in the famous Opera, "Aida" so we rehearsed most evenings. One of the singers in the Opera took a particular interest in me. Her name was Angela, she was married to Michele but they had no children. Every day she made sure we spent some time together. Encouraging me in my dancing she made me even more enthusiastic about the stage. I felt guilty for accepting her affection and attention, especially when sometimes she would ask if I would like to live with her and her husband.

They desperately wanted a child but for some reason were unable to achieve their desire. After all the longing for my mother, I could not entertain the thought of ever leaving her again. Yet it felt nice to have people who cared enough to consider adopting me. Angela would discuss with me my possible future on the stage. She pointed out how she and Michele could afford to send me to a private school and how, someday, I might become famous. I found this prospect exciting but could not bear the thought of being separated from my mother again.

Angela took it upon herself to write to my mother. She put the proposition to her and waited for her response. Mother sat me down to discuss the letter, pointing out how I would benefit from a better life with Angela and Michele. For her part, however, she said she could not bear to lose any of her children. Her hope was we would all, one day, be reunited with our father and be able to live as a proper family again. She made it clear that the decision had to be mine. The response to Angela and Michele, therefore was no!

From time to time, especially when money was tight, mother would mention the letter and wonder if she was being selfish by denying me a better life. I assured her that nothing in the world would make me leave her.

The opening night at the Opera House in Bergamo arrived. The singers were from the Milan Opera Company who usually performed at La Scala in that city. We dancers were "Children of the Court" we were very nervous. Each of us had been given two tickets for members of our family to attend the performance. I cannot begin to describe my excitement. We were dressed as Egyptian children in colourful clothes, our faces were blackened and we wore curly wigs.

The show lasted for two weeks. It was a huge success. Seeing my mother sitting near the front with tears of joy in her eyes, I felt so proud that, at last I had achieved something. I may not have been famous but I had performed on the stage in front of a large audience who, apparently, liked what they saw. When the Opera came to an end. The cast moved on. I had a very emotional parting from Angela but I never saw or heard from her again.

Chapter Nine

The war seemed to be getting closer to us every day. Almost every night the siren sounded and we sought shelter while the bombing raids took place. Signs of stress were apparent. Almost everyone had a loved one involved in the war in one way or another. We were, I suppose, lucky that our father was in North Africa and not in the forces fighting here in Italy.

It was during this period that Lucia's mother received a telegram informing her that her eldest son had been killed in the line of duty. This was a very sad time for my friend, her mother was so overcome with grief that she barely acknowledged Lucia's existence, so I spent much of my time with her. Her brother, Paolo of who, by this time, I had become extremely fond of, was also devastated by the death of his brother.

Some three months passed with longer and longer periods being spent in the air raid shelters. Nobody went out at night because of the dangers. Many Italians were, I discovered, against the Germans. These "Partisans" had formed themselves into clandestine groups, hiding in the hills during the day but raiding German positions after dark and killing any German soldiers they came across. Eventually these raids became so frequent and successful that the Germans put up posters everywhere that said for every German soldier found dead ten Italians would be shot.

While I attended dancing school, mother often took Marcello, Emanuele, Pina and Antonietta for a walk through the woods where they hoped to collect wild vegetation, which would be good enough to eat. We were used to root soup, pies with unknown berries. We never knew what we were going to eat next, but there was an air of adventure and competitiveness in discovering edible vegetation growing wild. We would not have been able to survive without the help of nature providing us with food. We often wondered if we would eat something poisonous. Something that would make us very ill or even kill us but this never happened, sometimes there would be a slight bout of sickness but nothing more drastic.

On one particular evening when I was spending time with Lucia in her home there was a very loud knocking at the door. Lucia and I ran to open the door where several German soldiers looking very stern and severe confronted us. "Where is the man of the house?" shouted one of the soldiers, in broken Italian. Lucia called out to her mother. Paolo, hearing the shouting, also came to the door. This was the biggest mistake of his life; two of the soldiers seized him and dragged him out of the house and down the street. No explanation was given. The young man was just taken.

What could Paolo possibly have done to receive this kind of treatment? He was only eighteen years old, one of the nicest, kindest boys you could ever wish to meet. He supported his mother and sister in every way he could and had now been taken from them by force to nobody knew where. Lucia's mother was hysterical, screaming, crying and in a total state of confusion. Lucia and I joined in the crying, guessing, by the way he had been taken; he was not likely to be treated kindly.

There was no news of Paolo's whereabouts for several days; he seemed to have disappeared completely. Lucia's mother called at the police station and approached a Major in the Italian army to try and find out what had become of her only surviving son. The answer was always the same "Sorry Signora Valle, we have not been informed by the Germans as to what they do with the men they arrest".

She was advised to look at the posters in the square as the Germans put up a list of names of Italians shot in revenge for each German soldier that had been killed. Two weeks of anguish followed and then Paolo Valle's name appeared on the list in the square along with the names of nine other men, all had been shot in reprisal for the killing of one German soldier. Paolo had not had any connection with the Partisans, but examples were being made to show that the Germans would not tolerate their soldiers being killed.

The pain and tragedy of Signora Valle and her daughter, Lucia was profound. Lucia and I became even closer, I shared her unhappiness and my mother tried to comfort Signora Valle as she had become very depressed and sometimes confused. The shock of losing all three male members of her family was very hard to bear. Lucia also was affected; she became pale and lethargic and had a cough, which never seemed to leave her. She would sometimes stay in bed and refuse to go to school. This was unusual for her.

I had always admired her and been a little envious of her beauty. Lucia and I began to argue over silly little things. I felt I was always the one who had to give way, as I felt sorry for her because her life was so unhappy now. I too was grieving, however, for, as I have said, I had grown very fond of Paolo. Then one day we had a serious disagreement. Being proud and stubborn I was determined that this time I was not going to be the one to make it up, I would not give in. So I decided to stay away from Lucia for a while and anyway it was depressing me seeing her mother continually crying.

The sun had completely gone from their household and it was affecting my concentration both at school and dancing classes. Some time passed and I grew more and more disappointed that Lucia had not sought me out. I also became more determined than ever that I would not make the first move. Lucia was not attending school or dancing classes and I wondered if she was all right. Occasionally I was tempted to knock on their door, just to reassure myself that everything was all right but then my pride would get the better of me, and I would walk on by.

Then one day Signora Valle knocked on my door. She spoke in whispers to my mother and then they called me over. They asked me if I would go and see Lucia. My reply was adamant "No, why should I? She should come to me, she caused the argument in the first place". They pleaded with me "Please Santina, go and see her, she is ill in bed, the doctors say she could die". "No!" I didn't believe them, they were trying to trick me into giving in. I stopped and thought for a moment, she had looked pale and had not attended school for a while, could this be true? I ran to her house as fast as I could and into her room.

Lucia was lying in a double bed; she looked so small, so pale and so ill. I flung my arms about her "Please forgive me" I pleaded. "I didn't know you were ill, why didn't anyone tell me? I thought you were just being stubborn". I asked her what was wrong but she didn't know, only that she felt very ill. Something told me that things were very wrong, her eyes stared at me, she was holding my hand and was desperately trying to say something. Realising how difficult it was for her to speak I asked her if she wanted me to talk about the good times we had had together. She smiled and nodded weakly. I began recounting the day in May when I had been feeling very down. This was because of the war and worrying about my mother and her health. Lucia had come to the door and asked if I would go for a walk with her. We had decided to go to the woods, as we loved it there. We picked wild strawberries and the ground was covered with wild cyclamen. We fantasised and danced among the flowers. We were two angels who had lost our way and been turned into two beautiful fairies. As we danced we went further and further from our homes without realising it.

When we felt tired we sat on a large stone dreaming. We promised we would always be the best of friends and nothing would ever come between us. We were as dear to one another as sisters. We went on again, not realising we were walking still further away. Then we suddenly heard the sound of the sea, we were puzzled. We ran towards the sound and there was the most wonderful sight, palm trees swaying in a gentle breeze and the gold of the sand contrasting with the background of deep blue sea. We were both enchanted and thought we were in paradise. All around was peace and serenity. We could not hear a human sound only the sound of the sea and the trees.

I looked into Lucia's eyes and said, "Dearest Lucia, if that was Paradise, you have nothing to worry about", she smiled at me and squeezed my hand. I could see Signora Valle in the doorway watching us and tears were running down her face. Somehow I felt that life was going to give her another cruel blow. My heart was aching for them both. I secretly hoped this was all a bad dream and I would wake up and everything would be as it was. Surely God would not be so cruel. I prayed and prayed. "Dear God, please save my friend her mother needs her. She has already lost her husband and two sons; she has nobody left in the world apart from Lucia. Please God don't let me down now".

Lucia appeared to get a little better over the next couple of days. Money was very scarce therefore doctors could not be called. The hospital had given Signora Valle some medication but told her there was nothing they could do for Lucia. She was terribly ill and only a miracle would save her. Nobody seemed sure as to what was wrong with her, Tuberculosis was mentioned, also the possibility of a blood complaint. Once again Lucia started to deteriorate, she was unable to communicate only her blue eyes gave any sign of life. She died peacefully at ten o'clock one morning. I will never forget the expression on Lucia's mother's face that morning.

She gazed up at the large wooden crucifix, which hung on the wall over the bed. Suddenly she snatched it from the wall and smashed it to the floor, where it broke into pieces. She was screaming and crying as she did so, she had completely lost her reason. Had she become deranged due to the tragedy of her life. The doctor had to be called, and Signora Valle was admitted to a hospital for the mentally unstable. She had lost all her family and been overwhelmed by her grief. We were all in a state of shock. My mother had to make the arrangements for my friend's funeral. It was a very sad time for all.

Lucia was buried without any family presence, only my family and some neighbours were there and the flowers were few. We could not afford them. I decided to place my dancing shoes alongside hers on the top of her coffin. I had no enthusiasm for continuing dancing any more. I lived in somewhat of a daze for the next few months. A whole family had disappeared. Where was God's compassion? My faith was floundering; I found every excuse not to attend church. Lucia's grave was quite close to the road I travelled to and from school. Each day I stopped and talked to my dear friend. Somehow I felt more at peace afterwards. All my family had to undergo tests to ensure we had not been infected by whatever it was that had killed Lucia. We were all given a clean bill of health, even me who had been so close to her all that time. Lucia's death had a profound effect on me. Despite the grief of her mother and my prayer to the almighty, he had stood aside and let this happen. God and I had fallen out!

Chapter Ten

Mother decided that we should move once again, I was not sorry but the thought of leaving Lucia's grave with no one to visit it or tend it gave me cause for anxiety. The war was getting fierce and danger was all around. We made our way further north. Part of our journey was by rail or by begging lifts on Lorries. A great part of our journey was made on foot, luckily we did not have many belongings left to carry along with us.

We had no destination but, arriving in San Remo found there were several empty houses and apartments as many people had fled the area. It was not difficult to find rented accommodation here, so we stayed. We tried to continue our lives but found it very difficult under our present circumstances. Each day we heard of more and more people being killed. I was still numb with grief at the loss of my friend and nothing seemed real anymore.

Mother, however, soon made friends. People were very good to us and in return we tried to help one another in whatever way we could. Some of the farmers would give us potatoes or vegetables in return for small jobs done around the farms. Marcello and Emanuele used to call on a daily basis to see if they could help in return for food.

We settled into new schools, Marcello was doing extremely well and the teachers were very pleased with his work. It is difficult to understand how he managed to study as much of his spare time was taken up trying to earn some food or money. I drifted from day to day, dancing school being no longer available to me and this made me sad.

I spent a great deal of time day dreaming of those idyllic early years we had spent together as a family in Libya. They were the beautiful years, before all the hardship, cruelty and long hard struggle to survive. The fact that mother was now with us did make a difference and certainly helped me to keep going.

Occasionally, I would think back and wonder what had happened to those few friends I had made in the school with the "vigilantes". Teresa often came to mind, I wondered what had become of her, would I ever see her again? I wondered too if she would ever get over her terrible experience at the hands of the gardener? The full extent of her assault was never investigated and life went on as if nothing had happened. The only good thing to come out of the situation was the fact that she was reunited with her sister Rosetta who would hopefully be able to support her.

Gradually we settled down and our lives seemed happier here. One day mother told us we were to receive a special visitor who would help us with food supplies and attempt to help us to return to our father. Our visitor duly arrived. He was a tall handsome man wearing the uniform of an Italian Army Officer.

Mother introduced him to us as Major Matteo Navaro, but we could call him Uncle Matteo. We took a liking to him instantly; he was gentle and seemed a very kind person. He talked to us at length about his children whom he had not seen for a long time and whom he missed terribly.

He began to visit us frequently, bringing us food, fruit and treats of sweets. I think our feelings were that this was someone sent from Heaven. I was not sure of his relationship with my mother but we never saw anything to suggest any intimacy between them. My brother, Marcello, however, began to feel that "Uncle" Matteo had started to replace our father and although he did not express these feelings his resentment was obvious. Whenever Uncle Matteo visited, Marcello's actions spoke volumes.

The visits from Matteo Navaro continued for several months and life was much easier for us all, we did not go to bed hungry, unable to sleep like we had done in the preceding years. Then mother complained of feeling unwell. I became anxious remembering that she had a heart condition. She promised to visit a doctor whilst we were at school.

At midday my sister and I were summoned to the headmistress's office and told that mother had been admitted to hospital. As there was no one able to take care of us we were to be sent to an orphanage. I was stunned, were events about to be repeated? Why when things had seemed so much better did something like this have to happen? I began to believe that god was uncaring and was allowing yet another disaster to fall upon us. I was also afraid for mother, what if she died?

Once again we were split up. Our youngest sister, Antonietta, was taken in by a friend of mother's but my sister Pina and I were admitted to an orphanage and my brothers again had to go to another. I worried constantly about mother. No one asked us if we wanted to visit her or indeed informed us of her condition.

My memories of the orphanage are limited, I can recall a circular building with a rose garden at the centre, and there was an archway, which led to a fountain and a statue of a little boy. I remember this because I spent most of my time in this part of the garden, not in play; play was something that did not figure very much in our childhood. We just seemed to stumble from crisis to crisis.

This small garden was, at least peaceful, despite the number of children. In the quiet my thoughts would wander, sometimes back to the country of our birth. I cursed the day we agreed to go on this supposedly wonderful holiday. Sometimes I would lose myself in thoughts of what life might have been like if I had been adopted by Angela and Michele. Would I now be on the road to becoming a great dancer?

I would then return to reality with a start. I would also wonder about what had happened to Matteo who having been an almost daily visitor, suddenly just disappeared from our lives. Eventually our mother recovered and we were able to return to her. I asked her what had been wrong with her and she answered that her illness was due to stress suffered over the past few years. Dear mother, she did have the responsibility of five children as well as herself to feed and care for, it was too much for anybody in such hard times. On my way home from school, shortly afterwards, I was stopped by one of the neighbours who asked how my mother was. She asked if mother was now feeling better and if she had lost the baby. I was confused, what was she talking about, what baby? The woman realised that she had said more than she should have and quickly turned and hurried away. I ran home and confronted my mother; her reply was that some people could be very malicious. The subject was never again discussed. Mother discharged us again from the orphanage.

As soon as we were trying to get back to a stable way of life another hurdle would present itself. Money was very scarce and mother found it difficult to pay the rent. We started to search for a cheaper apartment and eventually moved into one with only two bedrooms. We three girls and mother shared one bedroom and the boys shared the other. We were very cramped and with five children it was sometimes chaotic, but we were happy again. Even though our supply of food was meagre, mother used to divide the daily ration into three meals, two meals were bread and a little cheese the third meal was a thin soup made from vegetables.

Chapter Eleven

The war was now more apparent and we again spent a great deal of time running to the air raid shelters. No sooner had the all-clear siren sounded than the warning siren of an impending raid would fill the air. Our fears grew and it was decided that perhaps it would be safer to take refuge in a disused railway tunnel nearby.

We gathered up our most treasured possessions, which were a photograph of our father and one of our grandparents. With some blankets and towels, to give us some comfort, we moved into the tunnel. With each day that passed, more and more families moved into the tunnel, some having lost their homes in the latest bombings. Eventually there were more than two hundred living there.

The Red Cross set up a small centre in the tunnel and supplied one meal a day. Several yards from us was another disused railway tunnel full of families living as we were. The tunnel became our whole lives and once again the feeling of being cut-off from reality and the rest of the world enveloped me.

It was during this time that we were able to talk at length with my mother. There was so much I wanted to know. Mother told me of the difficulties they encountered living in Sicily, how, even though my father's employment was reasonably well paid and secure they longed for a different life style.

It was for this reason, when the government began publicising the opportunities to be had in the colonization of North Africa that my parents began to think of leaving Sicily. This, of course was before they were married. At this time they were planning their marriage under the auspices of their two families.

Reports of the difficulties encountered by those who had gone to North Africa earlier were not too reassuring but the government insisted that changes had taken place. Initially, the families who went there were faced with arid desert conditions. Leaving their homeland, families and friends they had to contend with excessive heat, shortage of water and very little local sustenance. However, their hard work and determination created a virtual paradise of well irrigated land producing wheat and a variety of vegetables. This, of course, was mainly confined to the coastal strip and beautiful cities were built, Tripoli, Benghazi etc.

Thus it was, mother told us, she and father were married and immediately set sail for Africa. It was difficult for them – leaving their loved ones behind but at the same time there was the excitement of a new life. So this is how it all began for my parents, arriving in a new land full of hope for the future

My father had to take manual employment as construction work was continuing at a rapid pace. While, as a young couple they were housed in an apartment my father knew the houses they were building were to be allocated to families. These houses were built on the outskirts of the cities creating a modern suburbia. After several months of sacrifice the houses and roads were built and everything was ready for the families to be allocated their accommodation.

Families, like ours were allocated housing in the new suburbs of Tripoli. People were settling down to a new life and despite their various backgrounds a sense of community was established. Schools, churches and community centres were springing up throughout the country and the Italian population now had a sense of belonging.

Families were settled and growing, children were born and at last there was the feeling of achievement. This was what they had aspired to when they left their families and friends in Italy to colonise North Africa. Our own family were now happily settled and our life seemed idyllic.

Apparently, early 1940 advertisements appeared in newspapers, shop windows and poster hoardings inviting families to take advantage of a very generous offer from the country's leader "Il Duce". This was the offer to take children from the age of three upwards on a spectacular holiday to Italy.

The idea was to instil a sense of belonging to Italy – rather than North Africa – so that these children would not forget their roots. It was suggested that this period of three months would be ideal for the children to assimilate their native culture and afford them some opportunity to experience life in their homeland.

Nobody at the time doubted the sincerity of this proposition or questioned the motives behind a "holiday" for several thousand children at the government's expense. The propaganda that this was to reward the families for their hard work in building up the Colony to such a high standard was enough to convince the population that the motives were genuine.

It was only after war was declared and the children were already in Italy that parents became desperate to be reunited with their offspring Now it was that our parents became frantic as no news of our whereabouts was forthcoming. Officials, when approached, were off hand, fobbing people off saying everything was fine.

As the weeks passed, mother explained, and still no communication either way parents were desperate. More and more they bombarded local officials but the line seemed to harden as directives from those in power told of the necessity, for security purposes, that no direct communication could be allowed.

It was at this stage people began to realize the ulterior motives behind this "generous" gesture. The families who had emigrated to North Africa were not "died in the wool" fascists, they had not been subject to the relentless propaganda of their countrymen. While appreciating the opportunities provided by Mussolini in being able to make new lives in this colony, they were not supportive of the war.

It was only when mother came to Italy to find us that the real truth was apparent to her.

The children had been brought to Italy in order to indoctrinate them. Fascism was more important to the regime than family life. They thought nothing of riding roughshod over families and their emotions.

After this narrative from my mother, I realized the reason for the regime in the "schools" where we had been "educated". It was clear we were being groomed as the youth of fascism. To this day I shudder at the thought of what we might have become if the Fascists had been triumphant.

Chapter Twelve

Our life in the tunnel continued in the same tedious fashion. It was almost a month since we had been outside in the daylight. We knew it was for our own safety as the bombardment continued around us but that did nothing to resolve our boredom. We were anxious to live a normal life again – to be normal children!

One day I asked mother if I could go for a walk with a girl of similar age with whom I had become friendly. Her name was Luisa. The all-clear siren had sounded a little while earlier and my mother checked with the Red Cross workers that it would be safe to venture out. They reassured mother that we would be quite safe.

Luisa and I made our way up the embankment and followed a lane, which led into some woodland. There was a clear blue sky and the hot sun filtered down through the trees casting many shapes and shadows. The birds sang as they soared above us, how I envied their freedom but still this was a time for us alone. The world seemed to stand still nobody else existed, there was only Luisa and I. Time had slowed down and everything around us happened in slow motion.

Wild strawberries grew in profusion and we gathered them as we sauntered happily through the woods. The wild flowers were so colourful after the dark interior of the tunnel we could scarcely take in all the beauty. We decided to venture even further and made our way amongst the pine trees pretending we were in a magic garden. We stopped from time to time to examine more closely the flowers and the various insects.

Then I heard a sound I recognised, it was the sound of the sea and as we emerged from the woodland we found ourselves standing on a small beach. The warm sun on our skins and the pungent smell of the wild flowers mixed with the salt in the air was breathtaking. The gentle swish of the sea was music to our ears. We quickly removed our shoes and socks and dashed to the edge of the sea. We stood in the beautifully cool water almost in a trance.

As we explored the beach further we examined some weathered stones and driftwood worn by the sea. The wood was host to ants marching along their food trails and spiders who had woven their webs in the cracks to trap their prey. I felt I could have spent the rest of my life in this idyllic place.

Being so open I was reminded of our home in Africa where I had often spent time watching ants and other insects busying themselves in the sand. I realized how much I missed what was to me my homeland. Particularly the sense of space after having spent the last month in the confined space of the railway tunnel.

This was heaven on earth, how could life be so contrasting, where we had just come from was a living hell. Luisa and I paddled happily at the water's edge and lost all sense of time, we did not want to leave this wonderful place. The memory of this beach is imprinted on my mind forever and when I feel sad or depressed I picture myself in that wonderful place and somehow this brings calm and peace to me.

We eventually become aware of the sun going down and decided we ought to make our way back. We had not encountered another person in the whole time we had been exploring. We walked for some time unable to focus our sense of direction; we had wandered so much we could not remember which way we had come.

After walking for a very long time we found ourselves on a main road, this certainly wasn't the way we had come, we should have reached the embankment by now. We looked anxiously at each other as we realised just how lost we were. We became aware of voices coming from the other side of the hedge. I tried to peer through the hedge but my view was restricted. There appeared to be some sort of building.

In fact it was a very smart three storey hotel with well cared for gardens that had an appearance of past elegance. We decided we had no choice but to ask for directions. We entered the gardens, they were beautiful and so inviting. Rose bushes and a large variety of flowers were in full bloom and the perfume was intoxicating.

As we made our way up the driveway two figures emerged from the building, I was glad, as the prospect of entering the hotel did not appeal to me but, as we drew closer, I realised in horror that they were German soldiers. I froze in terror, my last experience of German soldiers had been when they had dragged my dear friend's brother Paolo from his home and shot him. I grabbed Luisa by the hand and started to run, faster and faster, to get out of the sight of these soldiers.

Someone shouted "STOP!" in Italian but we ran even faster, like two criminals. Luisa was gasping for breath but I would not stop. I stumbled and fell, my knees hurt terribly but no matter, I had to get up and we had to keep running until we were completely out of their sight. Dear God, don't let them catch us, especially today, after the wonderful experience we had had. We wanted to live to be able to experience it again.

We did not know in which direction we were heading, it could be that we were actually heading away from the tunnels and it was getting dark. I was exhausted and felt sure we were far enough away now to stop for a minute and catch our breath, I stopped for a moment and then realised that Luisa was not with me.

I was completely alone and frightened as to what had happened to Luisa and what on earth was I going to tell her mother if I ever found my way back to the tunnel. I hid in some bushes trying to see if I could see Luisa but it was too dark. My knees were very painful and were hot and sticky. I glanced down and realised my legs were covered in blood but I had to go on, this was a life and death situation. I would not allow myself to die at the hands of German soldiers.

I heard footsteps approaching and froze in terror. I peered cautiously through the bushes, a man was nearby and to my relief I realised he was an Italian. I emerged from the bushes, giving him quite a start and begged him for directions to the two disused railway tunnels. He tried to talk me into cleaning the blood from my knees and started asking too many questions, "I only want to know where the railway tunnels are," I said sharply. I felt like a rabbit needing to run to his warren for safety.

He then directed me to the only two tunnels that were within walking distance and I felt sure they must be the ones I was looking for. I started running again, as fast as I could, as I realised that my mother would be worried about me and possibly be looking for me. I had not expected such a wonderful day to turn into such a nightmare.

I then spotted the entrance to the tunnel, I ran inside and stopped to examine my knees, there was a large piece of glass protruding from the flesh of my right knee. I hurried to where my mother and siblings were and quickly hid under a blanket trying to cover both my legs. My mother was irate, asking me where I had been and what had I been up to. She sensed that something was wrong.

Within minutes of my return there was an announcement by the Red Cross over the loudspeaker "A little girl of about eleven or twelve has been seen running through the tunnel, she is bleeding severely from a leg injury, would anyone finding her please bring her to the Red Cross where medical attention will be given". I was in agony, the glass was still protruding from my leg and the wound was bleeding profusely, but I did not move.

My mother had not seen the state I had come back in as she had been facing the other way and I had hidden myself under the blanket. I thought, in my innocence, that the call was a trick on the part of the Germans to make me reveal myself. Mother kept looking at me, she knew there was something wrong but did not know what.

"Have you enjoyed your walk Santina?" "Yes thank you mother" I replied. "Are you all right?" I nodded my reply and she could tell by the expression on my face that I was possibly in some sort of pain. She pulled the blanket from me saying "Come, get up, if you sleep now you will not sleep later". I was virtually lying in a pool of blood, she screamed in horror, snatched me up in her arms and ran to the Red Cross emergency room. When I told her why I had been so afraid she cried with me. We then met Luisa's mother who was in a state of panic, asking me where Luisa was. I told her that we had somehow become separated when we were running away from the German soldiers. I had tried to look for her and had called her name several times but to no avail. After a search lasting about an hour, Luisa's brother came running into the tunnel saying he had found her; she was exhausted and was walking towards the entrance very slowly. Luisa then appeared and managed to run the last few paces into her mother's arms. She said that she had been very frightened as she did not know where she was. A lady, however, had shown her the way back to the tunnel. She could not find me and feared that I had come to some harm. We both learned our lesson from this experience and swore never to venture so far away from our families again.

Chapter Thirteen

Our lives in the tunnel continued, we were never sure if we would still be alive the next day. We became accustomed to sleeping on the hard ground. The hardest thing to bear was the constant dripping water from the tunnel roof and walls that by morning made our blankets soaking wet. Our only means of washing were two taps at the end of the tunnel, which provided us with a meagre trickle of freezing cold water.

One night we were woken by a loud explosion, which sounded, ominously close. Mother gathered us all close to her to protect us as there was a great deal of confusion and people were shouting and crying. What had happened? It emerged that further down the track, at the next tunnel, bombs had exploded at both entrances, killing all of the people that were sheltering inside.

Everyone seemed to have lost friends or relatives and we all realised it could so easily have been us. How does one console oneself when a tragedy like this happens? The war was now very real and we began to realise that sheltering in the tunnel was not any safer than being in our apartment. Mother decided that we should return to our apartment, at least we would have some home comforts.

She was now suffering from pain in her joints due to all the dampness we were experiencing from living in these conditions and she was worried that we children might suffer too. It was decided that we would take one day at a time. If the siren sounded and we could hear aeroplanes, then we would run for shelter to the nearest bunker.

However, one night, when the warning siren sounded, there was no time to leave for the shelter before the bombing started. We children huddled together, a violent tremor shook the apartment block, and windows and light bulbs shattered scattering glass everywhere. We were in total darkness and afraid to move because of the broken glass surrounding us.

We screamed and mother called to each one of us by name, reassuring us and telling us not to move. Mother then made her way as near as possible to us, touching us, kissing us and soothing our fears. It was at these times that she would call out for our father, as the responsibility for us and for our safety became too much for her.

When daylight came we surveyed the damage. Our apartment had been quite extensively damaged with every window shattered. The building opposite had been totally destroyed and the top floor in our block of apartments had been very badly damaged. Many people had been killed or badly injured.

We could hear cries and screams as people realised the extent of their loss, their beloved families or their homes and for some, both. Mother had suffered a few cuts and bruises as too had little Antonietta, who had slept through the siren, but then some glass had fallen on to her forehead which had startled her awake. We thanked God that at least we were all alive, together and safe, but the shock was having an effect on all of us.

Mother tried to find alternative accommodation for us but there were hundreds of people in the same situation. The task was impossible. We were also very short of food and mother found it increasingly difficult to carry on caring for us, not knowing where the next meal was coming from and now, our apartment was almost uninhabitable.

Mother tried to get help from the Local Authorities but none was forthcoming. She was advised to place us, yet again, in an orphanage. "Please God, don't separate us from our mother again!" was my immediate reaction. We left the city and made our way to the hills, we were searching for some kind of shelter, anywhere, so that we could be together.

I kept looking at mother; she was tired and fraught had aged a great deal over the last few months. Her search until she found us all had taken its toll. She was now finding it increasingly more difficult, to complete her task of reuniting us with our father in order that we would once again be a complete family. Mother was aware of my constant watch over her and she said "Santina, I love you all dearly and will do my utmost to keep you together, but I also want you all to be safe until this war is over. Please forgive me if I have to put you once again into an orphanage, but I will not be far away and will not ever lose you again." Tears were running down my face, mother was crying too. My brothers and my sisters joined in and we cried unashamedly as we hugged together. We stayed like that for a long time. I believe my mother was feeling very guilty and yet had no alternative, if we were to survive. Eventually we came upon a convent and our mother begged shelter. The Nuns agreed to care for us children and allowed mother to remain with us for a few days until she could find accommodation for herself. This it was felt would be easier than seeking a place for six of us. In order to accept, once again, separation from our mother, I rationalised that it would give her opportunity to rest. She was looking very pale and tired in her anxiety. There was, however, still a sadness in my heart, when would it all end?

Chapter Fourteen

We settled into a routine once again, but found some difficulty with our schoolwork, as it had been several months since we last attended school. The Nuns were of a strict religious order and one of the rules was, that we must face the wall when dressing or undressing, as we must never allow others to see our bodies. This instruction made a lasting impression on me, and to this day, I find it difficult to undress or dress in the presence of others.

I became withdrawn during this period of my life and found it difficult to communicate I did not speak unless I had to. The Nuns were concerned, constantly asking me if I was ill, they said I looked pale. Parting from our mother was having a noticeable effect on all of us. I also lived in fear of what the future held, I could not see things improving. While the war continued our father could not send money how would we survive.

Mother did keep her promise to visit as often as she could. On one occasion, after mother's visit, I remembered the prayer I had learned years before. It had been answered we were reunited with our beloved mother. Could it possibly happen again? Every night I knelt at my bedside and prayed the fighting would cease.

Since witnessing Lucia's mother smashing the crucifix and proclaiming it was evil, I had neither prayed nor attended church. Yet in my heart, I knew I believed in God. I had spent much of my childhood surrounded by Nuns and had been influenced by their faith. Weeks passed and I repeated my prayer every single night. Rumours began to circulate that the war was coming to an end. It was now 1945, there was talk of surrender. God was listening to me again, there was something in the power of prayer after all.

Mother visited a few days later, she would bring us up to date on what was taking place in the outside world, but on this occasion it was different. I will never forget the expression of joy on her face. She said it had been announced on the radio about an hour ago that the war had ended. Germany and Italy had surrendered. We all jumped for joy. It was the 8th of May 1945

The Nuns had heard only the previous rumours as radios were not allowed in the convent and as yet, nobody had told them. Mother Superior made a telephone call and confirmed the joyous news. Mother told us she would try to contact relatives in Sicily perhaps we could make our way there. It would be easier to travel across the sea to Tripoli from Sicily and join our loved ones. Accordingly she wrote to her family in Sicily but had no idea how we would get there. Even if we did manage to travel to Sicily we still had to find a way of getting to North Africa.

It was two months before an answer to mother's letter was received. Her four sisters and two brothers, who were all living in Sicily, were relieved that she was safe. They indicated that they would do all they could to reunite us with our father. We started making plans to travel from the north of Italy to the south. We had no money and very little in the way of belongings.

The Nuns offered to help us with food and clothing and said they would also approach the church to see if some money could be donated to help us on our way. Time was passing and I was becoming very impatient. The war had been over for six months but things were still moving slowly. We were not living with our mother and the various officials mother contacted were of no assistance to us. Our return to North Africa seemed no closer.

The Nuns managed to obtain some help from the church and food and clothing was provided for our journey to the South. It was now November and we had to leave before winter set in. On a gloriously sunny day we bade farewell to the sisters and set off, not without some feeling of trepidation. In order to save what little money we had, we sought lifts from passing traffic. It was a difficult task, very few drivers wanted to take on board a woman with five young children.

We walked miles, following a map that had been given to us by the Nuns. Although it was hard and very tiring, we were filled with the prospect of our future together. It was, too something of an adventure. After being confined in for so long we children were excited and looking forward to the prospect of being reunited with our extended family. We met several other families who were also trying to reach relatives and friends further south. They had travelled northwards to escape the dangers of war as the Allied Forces advanced.

Evening approached and we had failed to persuade one single driver to give us a lift. We had only travelled some ten miles on this first long day. The journey looked like it was going to take forever. We found shelter in an unused railway station and settled down for the night. We huddled together to keep warm; it was difficult to fall asleep on a hard cold floor with only our coats to keep us warm.

During the night I heard scratching noises coming from a corner of the room, it was very dark and impossible to investigate. I froze with fear, I called out to my mother, as I shouted I heard a scuffle, something was running away. I was convinced we were sharing the shelter of the station with rats and this was confirmed the next morning when we discovered several of our belongings had been chewed up. I was glad we were leaving.

We called at a farm to buy some milk. The farmer and his family were friendly. They offered us fruit when they heard about our journey and we were most grateful. Again we started to walk and encountered many families undertaking the same journey of hope. We made friends with two sisters who jointly had six children, they wanted to tag along, but the prospect of getting lifts with eleven children and three adults were not encouraging. We therefore had to walk separately and hope that each family would be lucky.

After what seemed a lifetime we stopped at a lay-by with a park at the side. Mother was very tired and looked ill, we begged her to spend the night here as we, too were very tired. Sleeping on the hard ground was becoming very uncomfortable we thought the grass looked much more inviting. Having toilets and washing facilities nearby was a luxury. Mother was eventually persuaded she seemed relieved but also concerned that we would be losing time in reaching our destination.

The thought of having food and accommodation for us was obsessive and she did not want to waste any more time than was necessary. We allowed ourselves the freedom of play, running wild, before we washed and settled down for the night. As I was lying in the luscious grass I was deep in thought as to what had happened up to now. I began to realise how much of our childhood we had missed, especially my younger siblings.

I recalled talking to Emanuele who could not recollect much of what had happened to him from the day we left home. One incident, however stuck in his mind. He remembered going with a friend beyond the fence, when they lived in the large home for boys. They were very hungry and had spotted some peas growing on the other side of the fence. They both decided it was worth the risk to steal some of the peas as the prospect of food outweighed the wrongdoing. They filled their pockets and inside their shirts with the pea pods. They then returned to their side of the fence where they were met by another boy who informed Emanuele that the Headmistress wanted to see him.

Panic set in, he could not understand why he was the only one getting into trouble for stealing the peas. He handed the peas to his friend and made his way to the head's office. He was crying, he felt that life was very unfair. He knocked on the office door, and the voice of the Head instructed him to enter. An office full of people faced Emanuele. He was confused and said, "I'll come back later". "No don't go," said the Headmistress, "I have a surprise for you." Emanuele was confused, the head's voice was kind and she was smiling. "Do you recognise one of these ladies?" She asked.

He saw two ladies, both of a similar age, neither was familiar to him. He was puzzled and thought, "Am I supposed to know them?" He waited for some signs or clues as to who they might be. One of the ladies smiled at him, he smiled back. "Your mother has come to see you" the Head said, "Give her a kiss" Poor Emanuele, he did not recognise his mother. Remembering that one of the ladies had smiled at him, he decided that this one must be his mother. He slowly made his way towards her; he took her hand and leaned towards her. "No, I am your mother", said the other lady. She embraced him and kissed him. Emanuele was confused and embarrassed. He was five years old when he last saw his mother, he was now eight, and could remember little about his past life. To his mother it was heart breaking to see her young son had no memory of her. She broke down, her friend and the Headmistress tried to console her. Emanuele told me years later, this was the only recollection he had of his childhood years between leaving Tripoli and returning to the family home there.

I had to force myself to think of the happier times there would be when all the family were together again. I fell asleep huddled close to Pina, who was now nine years old. We always slept wrapped together for comfort. For two years we only had each other. Somehow we could blot out every upsetting feeling when we embraced. We did not feel that we were sleeping on cold and damp ground; we only felt it when it was time to get up. We were stiff and aching all over.

I worried about mother, this dampness was not doing her any good but she never complained. All the families we met were walking in silence, carrying their pitiful bundles of belongings. We managed to get a lift twice in one day and it took us some 200 kilometres nearer our destination. The next day however we were not so lucky, there were no lifts and we had to walk all day. It was very late at night but despite our exhausting day. Mother insisted we should go on.

There seemed a sense of urgency about her, as if time was running out. We complained bitterly, we wanted to rest, the younger children were crying, they were hungry. Mother agreed we could rest on the pavement, she was hopeful of another lift. I curled up on the pavement and fell into a deep sleep. Mother shaking me roughly interrupted my sleep.

A lorry driver had stopped and offered us a lift. He was becoming abusive saying, "Do you want a lift or not, I can't waste time" Mother was in a state of panic,' Please children wake up, we can't afford to miss a lift, tomorrow we might have no offers at all'. We all rose quickly, picked up our belongings and climbed on this huge lorry. The driver insisted that Mother should sit in the cabin with him; he said she would be more comfortable there.

Mother did as he suggested, but Marcello felt uneasy about this driver.. After a time the lorry suddenly stopped, the lorry driver ordered us to get down, saying "Find another fool to give you a lift, especially with five children". Mother was very upset. Marcello told me later that he had seen the driver trying to molest her. Mother had resisted his advances and told him to stop the lorry.

Once again we were looking for somewhere to rest, we found shelter in an old ruined church, and settled there for the night .It was very cold and damp, we had not slept in a bed for a very long time, We were beginning to feel desperate and absolutely unwanted. It was another two weeks after this when fortune smiled on us.

We had reached a small place called Villa San Giovanni in the south of Italy when we met up once again with our former friends, the two sisters and their children. They also looked exhausted and unkempt. However, they had made contact with the owner of a small fishing boat and he was prepared to ferry them across to Sicily. They introduced mother to this elderly boat owner and he agreed to take us as well.

We eventually boarded the boat, it stank of fish but we were more than grateful for the owner's kindness. He was like Father Christmas such a jolly man although he continually cursed Mussolini and the "stupid" Italians who had taken Italy into the war. He said it was the least he could do to help the unfortunate enough to have suffered because of the war.

The journey was short but pleasant and we were landed in Sicily at a place called Torre Faro. This is in the north of the island and we still had to travel down to Gela where mother's family lived. The two sisters also were anxious to return to Tripoli so we were all travelling together once again. Mother was much happier to be back in Sicily and her health seemed to have improved too.

Our journey through Sicily was much pleasanter and we were given lifts on large lorries which meant we reached Gela in just two days. Our friends the sisters asked if mother could, through our relatives, obtain for them accommodation for a short period. They hoped they too, could arrange their return to Tripoli, back to their husbands and extended family.

While she wanted so much to help, mother felt that our problems were enough to burden our relatives with. We finally arrived; many aunts, uncles and cousins who were all strangers to us welcomed us. They were, however, very pleased to see us. Most of our aunts had not seen our mother since she left Sicily on her wedding day nearly sixteen years previously.

After our welcoming reception we settled down to our first hot meal for a very long time. There was very little room so my sisters and I had to sleep separated from our brothers and mother. This, however, did not upset us, we were grateful we no longer needed to worry where we would be able to find food or shelter.

Our relatives were also able to help with accommodation for our new found friends. Although it was a derelict farmhouse, it provided more shelter than they had been able to find during their long journey. They settled well there and we saw them on a regular basis until some four months later when they made contact with their own family and moved to be with them.

Chapter Fifteen

The family decided that longer-term plans had to be made as none of our relatives had a house big enough to accommodate the five of us together. It was difficult also for one family to feed us on a long-term basis. The oldest aunt could not help at all as she had ten children of her own. Her husband was a fisherman, and they were struggling on his small income.

It was agreed the two boys would eat and sleep in one household, the three sisters would stay with another maternal aunt and mother would stay with yet another relative. It become impossible to live as a family unit, but we will always be grateful for their support at this crucial time.

As time passed I became more concerned about mother, she was pale, listless and had lost a lot of weight. She seemed to be in pain, but never complained, some days you could see and feel that she was running a temperature. She was still writing to and visiting various departments where she thought help might be forthcoming in our desperate quest to be repatriated to North Africa.

No one would accept responsibility for our predicament or even acknowledge our existence. Despite the fact that it was the Italian Government who had brought us here in the first place! The answer was always the same," It will be at least a year before we can repatriate you or anyone else back home, there has been a war ". As if we did not know there had been a war. This made mother very angry, but she had a very urgent mission with no time to lose. She had to reunite us with our father.

Another six months passed. Only through the kindness of our relatives did we survive. It was very difficult for them as well. On occasions we turned up for meals to find only bread and olives left. At other times we were luckier and able to share cheese and very occasionally some meat. It was becoming clear that we had outstayed our welcome. Despite all the kindness shown by the members of our extended family, it was increasingly difficult for them to support us. The strain on everyone was beginning to show.

Mother became even more determined to achieve her mission - to see her family reunited. She was now showing real signs of illness. One of my uncles decided she ought to see a specialist in Palermo, the capital city of Sicily. He made all the arrangements through the family doctor who was puzzled by her symptoms and unable to diagnose the cause of her illness.

Uncle Rocco was in a better position than other relatives to pay for any medical visits as he had spent several years in America and saved a lot of money. He had returned to Sicily some five years previously and bought himself a fishing boat, which gave him and his family a reasonable life style. He felt, however, he had to conserve his money as he did not know what the future held. His family were kept on frugal rations too but they, at least, never went hungry.

It was a very generous gesture on his part, therefore to offer to pay for mother to be examined by a specialist. At the time I did not realise the significance - that mother was very ill. Aunt Maria and uncle Rocco accompanied mother on her visit to the specialist in Palermo. After a through examination the specialist diagnosed rheumatic fever. As mother had a weak heart, the prognosis was not good.

The doctor spoke of a new wonder drug recently discovered in Britain but only available in America. The drug was Penicillin, but the doctor had no idea how it could be obtained. It would obviously be very expensive. The doctor's diagnosis that mother's chance of survival was slim unless she could be treated with penicillin was like a death knell. He might just as well have suggested that we fly to the moon.

How could we purchase this drug, we did not have the money. Neither could we expect our family to be able to meet such an expense. Even if the money was available we did not know how it would be possible to obtain the drug. We just knew that mother was very ill and needed help. Mother's condition was now serious; her debility had increased alarmingly. She was so weak she was unable to leave her bed. Our relatives provided her with a more comfortable bedroom.

We watched anxiously, they spoke in low voices between themselves. I feel that, while they were deeply concerned by my mother's illness, they were also worried about the future of her five children. Who would accept responsibility for these children? We understood mother was very ill and needed a great deal of care but we also felt neglected, nobody seemed to care whether we ate or not. We were very much left to fend for ourselves. This was a worrying time, as we had no income at all.

We also knew that our relatives were struggling to keep their own families fed and clothed. I felt it my duty to accept responsibility for making sure that mother was always comfortable and that we five children had, at least, some bread every day. I arranged with the local baker that my father would pay the bill as soon as he could. I cut the bread into five equal parts, at least we could survive. Mother did always have one reasonable meal each day to keep her strength up, she was not aware of our predicament.

I took on the task of ensuring that we children washed ourselves and changed our clothes. I was only thirteen years old, but I was the oldest girl, someone had to take responsibility. I am not quite sure how it came about, we ended up sleeping in a cellar, but we were all together. This was a blessing in disguise.

The cellar was under the greengrocer's shop owned by my eldest aunt and was often used to store fruit and vegetables. We were able to eat a little of the produce and this made life a great deal easier. We had a double and a single bed, the three girls shared the double bed and the boys slept in the single. After making sure our mother was comfortable for the night, we went down into the cellar often quite early in the evening.

We spent a lot of time talking about the future, and occasionally talked about our life in Tripoli. The younger children remembered very little about Tripoli. We also discussed some of our experiences in the various children's homes. At these times Emanuele tried very hard to remember but he had set up a psychological barrier and was unable to recall anything. We sometimes cried and held each other tightly. We were aware that mother was very ill, possibly dying, we felt quite hopeless and helpless. We often wished our father could be with us, or at least help us obtain the penicillin that mother needed so badly

One night as we sat round the old table in our cellar we decided we had to do something, our mother's situation was desperate. We needed lots of money for the drug, I suggested we could perhaps rob a bank "No, no, we will go to prison" the younger ones said. "Well perhaps we could beg, or approach some rich people" the boys suggested, "It would not be so bad if we explained why we had to do this that our mother is dying and needed help." We talked for hours not knowing what to do.

A wild idea came into my head, sparked by the notion that we should approach rich people. Why not the King? He was a rich man and a very kind man. What could we lose? I was imagining this very powerful person of great wealth ordering one of his officials to go to America and bring the drug straight back to us. Yes, it was a big dream but I insisted it was worth a try and we decided to write to the King.

Putting the letter together was very difficult we had not had much education nor did we have any proper writing paper, but we were not deterred. "Dear King" we wrote, we explained how we had been moved from our home in Tripoli for a supposed three months holiday to Italy, This holiday had lasted almost six years.

We told how mother came to look for us after two years without any knowledge of our whereabouts not even knowing whether we were dead or alive. She had to come alone with our younger sister as our father had to stay behind. We explained how she had traversed Italy to find us. How, when she was successful in getting us all together, she sacrificed her health on our behalf. We told how often she did not eat in order to save money and how this had adversely affected her. She was now so ill we were afraid she was going to die.

Our feeling of desperation was transferred to the paper. How much we wanted our mother to get better and her dream of the family being reunited. We explained the specialist's recommendation that the recently discovered drug, penicillin, was really her only chance of overcoming her illness. How he had explained the drug was only available in America and was very expensive.

As we were not in any position to afford this medication or how to go about getting it, we wrote, "Please, Please, dear King can you find it in your heart to help us. It is very important to us; she is the dearest thing in the whole world to us. We are going to be alone if our mother dies; the youngest of us is only six years old and the eldest fifteen. We have no money and very few belongings. We cannot raise the money.

We pointed out that all our mother's sacrifice would have been in vain. I could not stop writing; there was so much to tell him. I felt that the King might be sympathetic. I was unburdening all my sorrow into this letter. It took several hours to write and rewrite the letter, it had to be right. Finally deciding we could not improve it further we went to bed. Next day we borrowed money for the stamp, we did not say why we had borrowed the money, this was our secret. After the letter was posted each day seemed like a month.

We were sure the King would not ignore our plea. Taking turns watching for the postman, we were all on edge. We had sworn each other to secrecy and made a pact that if and when the letter arrived it would not be opened until we were all present. The king had to help, we had no other hope. Our mother was going to die if she did not get the drug. I prayed every night; surely God in his mercy could not let this happen - we had suffered enough!

Two weeks went by, there was still no news. We occupied our time in the best way possible. The boys were attending school from eight in the morning till midday. My two sisters were also going to school for short periods, but I was not attending school at all. I did not have time to go to school, mother needed caring for. I had to make sure she was fed, washed and her bed made up. I had to be there for her.

Everybody else seemed to be preoccupied with his or her own homes and families. At the end of the day when mother was settled, I would try to give some time to the younger children. The boys were not so much of a problem, they occupied themselves playing football on the beach, they were football mad. The two girls needed me much more.

I valued this time with the girls, they had missed so much, and Antonietta was now six years old and Pina only nine. We did not possess any toys, our games were played with either five little stones or a skipping rope, and occasionally we had a card game. How I wished I could give them a toy with which to cuddle up at bedtime.

It was not very often they could have a hug from mother. When she tried to do this she suffered great pain, indeed she did each time she moved. This upset mother, she felt very inadequate. I tried to comfort her and told her the children were not missing out much as there were a lot of relatives. The truth was very different, most of the relatives were quite distant but, to be fair, they had their own problems.

Three weeks had passed since our letter was posted; we still waited anxiously for the postman but to no avail. We were becoming more and more despondent. A few days later a neighbour sought me out and told me a young man on a scooter was looking for me. I dropped everything and ran towards him. I was shaking all over, Could this be what we were waiting for? He greeted me and handed over a telegram, it read "Penicillin on the way, hope your mother will be well soon" it was signed by Prince Umberto, the King's son.

We could not believe it. There was justice after all. We kissed and hugged one another and ran to see our mother, waving the telegram. She was confused as she was unaware of our actions. When we explained she was in tears and kept on saying, "You are wonderful children I love you so very much"

News travels fast and the whole neighbourhood was curious to know what was going on. The telegram went from hand to hand. Suddenly everyone was interested in us. We called the doctor who came very swiftly. He assured us that as soon as the penicillin arrived, he would ensure a nurse was available to administer the medication and keep a record of mother's progress.

Two days later the long awaited medicine arrived by special delivery. The doctor himself administered the drug saying he'd decided he would personally monitor mother's progress. He told us only half the required dosage had arrived, however a note confirmed that the rest of the medication was being dispatched in time for the necessary full course of treatment to be completed.

Mother commenced regular injections; the doctor was very interested in the new drug. It was said to be successful in curing several illnesses and would be the drug of the future. This made us feel good, we were all now convinced that mother would recover. The doctor informed us that he would not charge us for his services, as he felt privileged to be administering a brand new drug. He was well aware that we could not afford his fees anyway.

Within three days there were signs of mother's improvement. Her temperature was falling and she appeared to be growing stronger. The doctor was very impressed with her progress. He was concerned however, that the second batch of the drug had not yet arrived, it was required within the next two days for the course to be completed.

We called at the post office where we were informed the parcel had gone astray. I could not believe what I was hearing. How could a parcel that the King had sent by special delivery go astray? Something was very wrong. However, the next day the parcel arrived, there was a great sense of relief.

The course of injections continued. Within twenty-four hours there was a different reaction to the drug. Mother was vomiting and showed signs of deterioration, what was happening to her? The doctor was confused; she had been doing so well. He felt that something was wrong so arranged for the drug to be tested.

We anxiously awaited the results. The doctor had a grave face when he told us the result of the test. This second batch was not the same as the first; in fact it was a drug, which was having an adverse effect on mother and undoing all the improvements achieved. How could this have happened? The doctor was very concerned and angry.

He contacted the Health Authorities in Palermo and an official enquiry was set up. It was a terrible shock when the police told us that during transit from America the drug had been substituted and the penicillin probably sold on the black market. The authorities never did find out how or where this substitution took place and who was responsible for it.

How could God have let this happen? The greed of man was responsible but surely God could have prevented it! We were devastated; all our dreams had been destroyed. Our mother's body was sapped of all strength we now knew for certain she was dying. How could anyone tell her that she had been robbed of her only chance of survival? What a cruel turn of fate, after all she had gone through. To be denied completion of her self imposed task of reuniting her family by unscrupulous criminals!

As her life slowly ebbed away my mother clung desperately to the hope that a way would be found to get us back to Tripoli or that our father would be able to come to Sicily. Mother continually asked if there was a way for us to return to North Africa, I pointed out that it was much more difficult to travel across the Mediterranean than to travel the length and breadth of Italy. She insisted that there must be someone; somewhere on the island that could help us, even if we had no money our father would pay them as soon as he was able to do so.

Chapter Sixteen

Because of her insistence I began to make enquiries of all my uncles, I was desperate to make my mother's dream come true. The same uncle, Rocco, who had so kindly paid for mother to be seen by the specialist, was again the only uncle to offer any hope. He said he would talk to a friend who owned a boat large enough to make the crossing to North Africa. Uncle believed his friend had successfully made a journey to Africa a few weeks previously.

He promised he would see him in the next few days. After a few days uncle Rocco informed us that his friend would be willing to take us to Tripoli but that we would have to pay for our passage before boarding. Without payment we would not be able to go. This meant mother would have to borrow money, as our meagre possessions would not raise nearly enough.

Although she was able, through our relatives, to sell everything we had of value, mother was not able to raise enough money to pay for all of us to go. In the evenings we children once again racked our brains trying to find ways of solving the problem. We were unable to come up with any solution and were left with the bitter realisation that only three of us could go.

To me it was inconceivable that three of us would have to stay behind but Marcello forced me to face the fact that this was the case. He rationalised that I should go to care for mother who was obviously too weak to care for herself and that Antonietta should go as she was the youngest. I knew he was right but I could not bear the thought of leaving my sister Pina who was only ten years old and who had been my constant companion for the past six years.

There was, however, no alternative so we went to mother telling her of our decision. She, of course, was devastated, she did not want her family split up again but was aware that she was unable to care for herself let alone her children. Our uncle was contacted and told we had sufficient funds to pay for three persons and, therefore, three of us would go. He said he would make the proper arrangements.

The boat was due to sail in the next few days but we must not say anything to anyone. This was because it was illegal to transport passengers in a deep sea fishing boat. On top of which the Authorities were not yet allowing anyone to travel to North Africa even those who had been born there. This has to be seen in context of the prevailing conditions. North Africa had been colonized by the Italians and opposing forces had occupied the country during the war. Obviously, Italians were not exactly welcome now.

The night before we were due to sail, the Captain of the vessel visited us. He had heard rumours of our mother being so unwell that she really was not fit to travel. He met our mother and it was obvious to him that she was extremely ill, he made the immediate decision that he would not take the risk of allowing her on board his ship. While expressing his regret that he could not help in this desperate situation, he was adamant.

He did not mince words. He said if she died on his boat he would have no alternative but to throw her body overboard. If this happened what would he do with two children who would no longer be accompanied by an adult. Despite all our pleas, the captain refused to change his mind and left to go about his business.

Naturally, we were all upset but mother was beyond herself with grief. My disappointment was tempered a little by the fact that we were all still together Once again my anger was directed at God. Where was he when we needed him? He was, we were told a great and loving God, why then were we destined to suffer so much, why did every plan go wrong?

Mother had perked up a little at the thought of returning to my father in Tripoli. She was sure he would be able to arrange the safe return of my brothers and sister as well. Now she seemed much weaker. Her pallid complexion worried me immensely. I knew in my heart that my mother was slowly sinking and that she would not be with us for very much longer, my heart was aching.

A few days later it was the 8th September. This is an important festival in the religious calendar. This is the day set aside to celebrate and give thanks for the Blessed Virgin Mary, Mother of Christ. All the churches in the province combine in a gigantic procession. The priests, bearing Icons, lead - followed by the men carrying the statue of the Blessed Virgin. All the girls are dressed in white and the boys wear dark suits and white shirts. Local bands march in the procession playing religious music.

When the procession reaches the sea front, the mood changes. The priests and the men deposit the icons and the statue in a shelter specifically arranged and then join the women and children. All along the front stalls have been set up, selling fruit and sweets. Various meats are cooked over open fires and there are sideshows and lots of games to play. The celebrations continue until dark when the day is rounded off by a magnificent fireworks display.

This custom is followed every year throughout Italy and most of the Catholic world, I am proud that it happens on my birthday. It was a beautiful day and I was looking forward to the festivities. However, I was still upset and angry feeling that God had deserted us when we needed him most. Realising that I had been named after the Mother of Christ made me suddenly think that I had been praying to the wrong person, perhaps in future I should address my prayers to the Blessed Mary.

Stifling my feelings I persuaded mother to leave her bed and watch the procession from the balcony. She made the effort because it was my birthday. Her thin frame was wrapped in a satin dressing gown and her skin was like alabaster. Despite her illness to me she was still an attractive woman and I felt any man would have been proud to call her his wife.

The gown she wore was quite an expensive garment, which had been a gift from the neighbours when they learned she was to have penicillin treatment. She was proud of this and always had it draped across her bed. We heard the sounds of the procession getting nearer, the music was tuneful and the children's voices sounded happy and excited.

Mother's eyes filled with tears, she embraced me and asked where the other children were. I told her they had followed the procession and hopefully would be able to join in the later festivities. Mother then asked me to find her a mirror she said, "Do you know Santina, I have not looked at myself in a mirror for nearly six months". My heart missed a beat, I was not sure this was a good idea; she had changed so much in the last six months.

I had no choice; mother had seen the hand mirror lying just inside the room. She lifted it in front of her face and her expression changed to a look of horror, "Oh God", she exclaimed, "What do I look like?" She turned towards me, her eyes again filled with tears. I threw my arms around her, crying silently with her, I tried to comfort her. She suddenly tensed, drew herself up so that she was standing quite erect and said, "I do not have much time left, I must take you all back to your father so that he can take care of you".

I tried to reassure her that there would be other opportunities. That now the war was over the Government had a duty to repatriate us to North Africa Mother then said, "I have not seen your father since I left Tripoli to find you, must I die without ever seeing him again?" I told her she must not talk of dying; we needed her and could not live without her! She must try very hard to get better for our sakes just as much as her own.

By this time mother was exhausted and I helped her back to bed. Once she was comfortable she told me I must go and join in the celebrations, after all it was my birthday. Despite my love for my mother and feeling that she should not be left alone, I was secretly pleased to be able to go and join my brothers and sisters. They appeared to be enjoying themselves and I managed to forget all the troubles and tribulations for a while and join in the fun.

The festivities were nothing like the usual celebrations as times were still hard. There was not the food or other merchandise available to provide the sort of celebration usually enjoyed on this day. However, we were able to have several games together and the boys and Pina went swimming in the sea.

My mother and all of us when we were reunited

My mother and I the day she found us

Chapter Seventeen

The scandal of the penicillin, mother's deteriorating health and our general predicament was the subject of gossip all over the town. As it was not a large town everybody knew everyone else's business. Since our correspondence with the King we had become something of celebrities. People expressed their sorrow when they saw us; others offered material help, which made our life easier.

All of this helped restore my faith in human nature, as, since the penicillin incident, I was not too enamoured of the human race. Every time I thought of a fellow human being having stolen the medication that could have helped my mother back to health, I felt so angry. A neighbour brought news that a farmer who lived some distance away, hearing of our circumstances said we could have food from his farm to help build up mother's strength.

That same afternoon, when the other children had gone to the beach and mother was asleep, I set out for the farm and the promised food. I walked for a very long time, it was very hot and I nearly turned back. I did not realise how far it was to the farm, I must have walked miles before arriving at the gate. The whole family made me very welcome. They told me to rest for a while, gave me a long cold drink. They were curious and wanted to know all about us.

Overwhelmed by their genuine friendliness I wanted to tell them everything that had happened to us but was conscious of the long journey that faced me. They would not hear of me walking back with the food they gave me and after a lovely home made pizza and another cool drink, the farmer's eldest daughter, returned me home in a small cart drawn by a donkey.

She did not come into the house but I ran excitedly upstairs to mother's room. I threw open the curtains shouting, "Mum, mum, look what I've got for you, you will soon get better now." Mother did not appear to be moving, I went closer she opened her eyes and tried to talk but no words came. My heart was racing; her face looked strange her mouth twisting to one side as she tried desperately to talk to me.

I knew instinctively that something was seriously wrong. I began to shout hoping I could attract the attention of an adult. Again and again I shouted, "Please, please someone get the doctor." An aunt, hearing me calling rushed into the room, realised something was drastically wrong and telephoned the doctor. He arrived within ten minutes by which time the room was full of people.

The two bags of fruit, eggs and vegetables, even the chocolate given to me by the farmer went unheeded on the table. The doctor cleared everyone from the room, apart from the aunt in whose house my mother was accommodated. He examined mother and said she had had a stroke and her condition was now critical.

My sisters, brothers and I were stunned. Even though we knew how ill our mother was this was a terrible shock. This was something different, we had not been prepared for this. Since her relapse we had seen mother fading slowly, but this was sudden and unexpected. She seemed so much closer to death now and this made us panic. Faced with this prospect of her imminent death we all went to pieces.

What would become of us, what would we do without our mother? The future was a blank, the outlook bleak. We sat by our mother's bedside holding her hands in turn. She looked at us intensely, we could see the pain in her eyes, she wanted to communicate and tried very hard to speak, the words would not come, She looked at each of us longingly her eyes rested on my face for what seemed a long time, I knew she was seeking reassurance.

I took her hand in mine gently squeezed it and whispered to her " Don't worry, mum, I will look after them, we will not allow anyone to separate us ever again, we will get back to father, I will tell him that, although you loved him, you had to find the children and this was the only reason you left" Mother inclined her head slightly and appeared to smile. She gave us all one last long look, closed her eyes and was gone forever.

Our dear mother was gone but her sacrifices will always be remembered. I was glad she was no longer in pain. It had been so hard over the past twelve months watching her suffering. We tried to alleviate her pain and suffering, but man's greed prevailed. While I was still angry with God for, what I considered was his failure to intervene I was sure he must now realise that our mother deserved to be among the Saints. That he would surely now ensure she enjoyed the peace she had earned through the sacrifices she made for her family.

I was grateful to my mother for her tenacity in seeking us out and reuniting us. If she had not, there is no telling where we would have ended. We sisters and brothers might never have been together again. At least we now had each other, although we were sad, unhappy and fearful of the future. Withdrawing to the cellar, which had become our haven, we hugged one another, there were tears but these were silent, neither was there a need for words. Each one knew how the other was feeling.

Although Marcello was the oldest, I knew it would be my responsibility to make sure we survived. It was a woman's role to care for the family. Our family was different from most in that our mother had been the sole provider since she had come to Italy to find us. This was not the fault of my father, as he could not leave his employment in Africa. The war prevented him from helping us in any way.

If there had been no stupid war none of this would ever have happened and our dear mother would still be with us. Our future, I felt, was precarious. While we were grateful for all that our extended family had done for us, it did not now seem that they were really very concerned about our future. Perhaps they felt our father should have made more effort to ensure our well-being but we knew this was impossible due to the situation and the aftermath of war. It is fair to say, that for this very same reason our aunts and uncles had their own problems, it was difficult even for them to survive.

Chapter Eighteen

As in all religious communities, Sicilians make a great effort to show their respect for the dead. There is, inevitably, a great deal of preparation for a funeral. All my maternal aunts were involved in preparing my mother's body for burial. I did, however, insist that her body be clothed in her satin gown of which she was so proud and which made her look so beautiful. She had lost so much weight; anyway that none of her dresses fitted.

The front parlour was cleared and mother's body was placed on a suitably draped trestle table. Candles were placed at her head and her feet and chairs placed around the room. This was for the family members to keep a vigil. It was insisted that all five children should be present. I complained bitterly, I felt my younger sisters were too young to cope with such an ordeal. We had experienced separation from our parents, the effects of war, our mother's illness and now her death. Our relatives reaction to her death and their apparent rejection of our feelings only added to our confusion, we were all in a state of shock.

My aunts were furious, they interpreted my attitude as one of disrespect for my departed mother. It was unheard of that children, regardless of their age, should be excused vigil at the side of their mother's body. I was not in a position to argue and reluctantly complied with their wishes. Their support was even more necessary for our future now than ever before. At this time I felt completely empty inside, I felt I had gone with my mother.

Despite these feelings I was aware of all that took place around me. I think I was in a state of 'limbo'. I was anxious, not knowing what the future held for us and of not being able to fulfil the promise I had made to my mother. Yes, I had been, in almost every sense, looking after my brothers and sisters for nearly a year but things were different now. There was no adult of our immediate family to intercede on our behalf. Our mother was dead and our father was far across the sea in North Africa.

My feelings of despair, anger, guilt and self-pity were such that I felt I just wanted to lie down and never get up again Our relatives appeared to be grieving but their grief did not seem to encompass us, I could not understand this. My brothers and sisters, who had seen me as the strong one during mother's illness again looked to me for comfort. But I was sadly lacking. I too, needed comfort, a strong shoulder to cry on, someone to embrace me and make me feel secure.

Although I had been aware for some time that my mother was losing her battle for life the reality of her death was so painful that I would not allow myself to accept it. As we sat in the eerie light of the candles, our relatives moaning and crying around us in the accepted custom we felt completely isolated.

We were not accustomed to this display of feelings. We had been through a great deal together and had supported each other with a quiet dignity my brothers sat stoically bearing their grief in silence, my younger sisters wept silently. I could only place my arms around them in an attempt to bring some comfort to them.

My mother's death had such a traumatic effect on me that suddenly I was gripped by a sense of fear which seemed to numb my whole being. I did not understand this feeling, how could I be frightened of something which was so intangible. Part of me does not want to know, I feel I should be screaming but I cannot. My reactions are automatic, I am not really responding to the adults around me. It is almost as though my life is on hold, nobody seems to be concerned about us, children who have just lost their mother.

Suddenly I feel this is too much for me, nobody seems to care. My mother was the only person who understood now she is gone. Although I am only thirteen I cannot give in to these personal selfish feelings. I have to be strong for my siblings. Despite my resolve to do this for them it is impossible for me to fully assume the role of mother. Trying to envisage the future for us without mother is a daunting prospect.

The following day the Undertaker arrived to collect mother's body. Again came conflict, my aunts insisted that all the children kiss mother before her body was removed. I protested, I wanted us to remember our mother as the warm soft person who gave us so much love, not as a cold, stiff body. My aunts were again angry, their culture did not allow for such inner feelings. There had to be a physical demonstration for them to be satisfied that we showed "proper respect". Anything short of this was misinterpreted as lack of feeling.

The day of the funeral was equally traumatic and I have to admit that I have blocked this out and do not, therefore, remember very much at all about that day. Following the burial, I seemed to be living in a daze. Although I was aware of my actions I did not seem to have any control over them. I was behaving completely out of character but could not help myself.

After seeing the younger children off to school I collected the dirty clothing for washing but I didn't wash them, instead I hid them. Everything seemed too much of an effort; all I wanted to do was lie down all day. I no longer had my mother to look after and, apart from my brothers and sisters nobody seemed to care about me at all.

Nobody came to see what I was doing and only when the teachers at school commented that the children appeared to be unwashed and their clothing dirty did anyone question my actions. My aunts could not understand my attitude they were indignant, I had let them down, I was supposed to care for my siblings. Their intervention had some effect on me and I made the effort to ensure the children were clean and properly clothed.

I had become obsessed with my mother's death; I felt that not nearly enough had been done for her. I wanted to vent my anger on everyone. I blamed Mussolini for the war and for taking us away from our parents and home under false pretences. I blamed my father for not being with my mother when she needed him most. I blamed my siblings for needing to be looked after and taking so much of my mother's health and strength. My relatives in Sicily I blamed for being uncaring and not doing enough to make sure she recovered. Most of all I blamed myself for not taking more of the load so that mother could conserve her strength and energy. My mother was gone, I could not accept this, the loss was too great. Despite feeling so depressed, I decided that I must pull myself together. My siblings needed me and there was nobody else to turn to. I turned my thoughts to our future and our return to Tripoli. At least there our life was pleasant and we were never cold and hungry. My father would be there for us, I tried to picture him in my mind, I could not remember. The younger ones must be even more confused as they are unlikely to remember very much at all about father and our life at home.

Chapter Nineteen

Three months passed after my mother's death but there was still no news from Government Departments about our possible repatriation to Tripoli. Despite the differences with our relatives on this island and our unease about our future, they did look after us. The day-to-day care of the family fell to me but our food and they provided and we must be eternally grateful to them.

Finally a letter arrived from our father; he was devastated by the news of mother's death. He was angry and feeling very guilty that he had been unable to be with his wife when she needed him most. His time, too, had been spent negotiating with the officials in Tripoli trying to resolve our situation. The officials there, however, were military personnel as the British Military Administration was administering the territory. There was an inordinate amount of 'red tape', which is not uncommon with the British.

Things were particularly difficult because the country was a former Italian Colony but the native Arabs wanted their country back. The future was so unpredictable that the British were loathe to allow any Italians back into the country. However, Father was able to prevail upon a British Major acquainting him with the details of his wife's death and the fact his five children were now alone in Sicily. The Major was sympathetic and arranged for father to transfer a substantial sum of money to Sicily.

Within two weeks the money arrived. We were so grateful and quite excited as we all needed new clothing and we were looking forward to clearing our debts and perhaps having a little left over for some of those things that had been so lacking in the past. Our relatives had a different idea. They felt that this money should be used to purchase a proper marble fascia for our mother's grave.

While we also wanted a proper grave to mark our mother's last resting place and be a fitting memorial to her we felt this was not the time. There were other pressing needs. We could not understand their reasoning. I tried very hard to convince them. We were still alive and more in need of the money for our creature comforts, than was my mother in need of a gravestone.

It was ironic that I who, only a short time previously, had been unable to accept my mother's death was now being realistic. It was of no matter, the adults had control of the money and they would decide how it would be spent. In Sicilian culture it is very important that the dead are shown respect this means the burial is important too.

Our mother had been interred in a temporary grave and this reflected on her family who had arranged the burial. It was, therefore, more important to them that they were seen to be doing the right thing in the eyes of the Church and their neighbours.

Arrangements were put in hand for mother's body to be disinterred and transferred to a zinc coffin which would then be placed in a proper 'wall grave' which is the traditional method of interment in Sicily. A service was arranged for the transfer to take place and all the families were invited to attend and witness the change over.

Again our aunts insisted that we children as the nearest relatives should be there. I could not believe what was being said. It was madness to expect children to view their parent's body so long after death. Once more I was accused of being heartless and unfeeling and told that no amount of argument would change their minds. I was distraught, how could I possibly prepare my younger sisters and brother for such an experience.

At least when she was originally prepared for burial she looked attractive, peaceful and at rest. I knew that to expose them to such an ordeal was wrong, whatever the priests said. I determined to try once again to spare my siblings this trauma. When my aunts were gathered together I appealed to them once again not to insist that the younger children attend. They could not understand why I was so adamant about this, saying that it would not be the first time children had witnessed an exchange of coffins.

I finally told them that if they insisted on the younger children being there none of us would attend the service. We would I said be a long way away from the cemetery and they would have to find us and take us there forcibly. They were not happy but did finally agree that only my brothers and I need attend. It was arranged for one of our cousins to look after my sisters as my brothers and I nervously prepared us for the ordeal.

None of us spoke, my mouth was dry and all three of us were fighting back tears. An uncle collected us, he did not speak either but he did squeeze my hand and gave me a reassuring smile. The journey to the cemetery was short but we wanted it to last forever, any delay would have been welcome. As we approached the cemetery, I closed my eyes, I said out loud, "God, don't let this happen!"

Nobody seemed to hear or if they did they ignored it. How could this be taking place, just as we were beginning to come to terms with mother's death, now this? I told my brothers to close their eyes; nobody could force them to look if they did not want to. All our aunts and uncles were there, most of our cousins and several more distant relatives. There were others whom we did not know, presumably friends of the family or friends who knew my mother.

I could not understand how these people could be so ghoulish, for to me that is what it was. They were all dressed in sombre black standing in front of the small church at the edge of the cemetery. Men, also dressed in black, brought the coffin, which had been dug up that morning, to the front of the church. The priest approached and led us into the church behind the coffin. A short service took place. All this time I cried silently and my two brothers held a hand each.

We left the church, again behind the coffin, the exchange would take place and then there would be the blessing. The time came for the coffin to be opened. The lid was unscrewed, my heart was pumping very fast, and I hugged both my brothers and managed to turn them so that they were not looking at the coffin.

It was not my intention to look either but some impulse made me look inside the coffin, as the lid was slowly raised. Perhaps I hoped that by some miracle my mother would look just as we had last seen her. I could see the bottom of the pink satin dressing gown and what appeared to be a stocking. I could not yet force myself to look further up the coffin to my mother's face, suddenly I saw something crawling inside the stocking, and I shuddered then lost consciousness.

The next thing I was aware of was someone calling my name and a wet cloth being put on my forehead. I was taken to sit in the church and my brothers were allowed to join me until it was all over when we returned home. This is an episode in my life that will remain with me forever.

For several weeks after this I was again in a state of suspension, my whole being seemed frozen. If it had been possible to withdraw from the world I would have been happy to do so. Nobody mentioned my fainting fit at the cemetery; I think my relatives were feeling a little guilty.

Life seemed to have returned to normal for everyone else but I could not rid myself of the sight presented to me. I was having nightmares and tried to stay awake at night in order not to experience the trauma again. One night, like any other, when I was dreading the recurring nightmare, I was so tired I fell into a deep sleep. This night, however, my nightmare did not return.

Instead, a dream came to me. I awoke to bright morning sunshine. I arose and went outside. It was a beautiful day, birds were singing but, strangely, there was no other sound. I had a feeling of being the only person in the world. I was mesmerised by the beauty around me, the sky was the deepest blue I had ever seen, and likewise the sea was an amazing colour.

Everything around me seemed to have more defined colours than usual. I had never seen the grass so green and there was an abundance of flowers. After standing there for what seemed an eternity I was overcome by a feeling of peace and serenity. Suddenly I was aware of something approaching from the distance, I could not identify what it was and there was no sound.

As it came closer I could see it was a black carriage pulled by four magnificent white horses but still there was no sound! No horses' hoofs, no sound of carriage wheels, no sound of any kind. The carriage came to a halt in front of me, but there was no coachman nobody was driving this carriage or guiding the horses. The coach itself was not ornate, but very plain and simple with the windows curtained so that it was impossible to see inside.

The door of the carriage slowly opened. I peered inside, there were two ladies sitting there, one dressed in black and the other in white, both wore veils. The lady dressed in white withdrew her veil to reveal my mother's face, I was taken aback but she looked so serene and lovely. I stared in disbelief as the other lady unveiled to reveal the face of my mother also she beckoned to me and called my name, "Santina come with me dear."

I was about to enter the carriage when my mother in white spoke, "Dear Santina, I am sorry, you can't come with us, you must look after your brothers and sisters. Don't worry, I will always be with you." The horses started to move off slowly and both figures waved as the carriage door closed. The carriage disappeared into the distance and I was, once again, alone.

I was not afraid and a feeling of peace and well being surrounded me. The next morning I awoke refreshed after a long night's sleep. The dream was vivid in my mind but I have never been able to explain or interpret its meaning. In my heart I am convinced that my mother knew how badly I needed comfort, guidance and support and this she gave to me in a very beautiful way.

This dream experience seemed to balance out the terrible times and the traumas I had suffered and gave me a new lease of life I was in control again and had to make sure that we made the best of our situation in order to take advantage of whatever opportunities presented themselves.

I felt a different person now. All the bad memories, the fear and even the pain had subsided. My siblings were amazed at this change in me, I made sure everyone was clean and well presented at all times, I was showing an interest in football and encouraging my brothers. They, of course, had always been enthusiastic about their football but I had not encouraged them at all seeing it only as causing dirty clothing and often cuts and grazes.

"Why have you suddenly changed? This was the question they all asked. I simply answered, "Don't worry, mum is watching over us, she will guide us whatever happens!" This was very real to me, whenever I had to make a decision I could almost feel her hand on my shoulder as I thought of a solution, I knew then that this was the right decision to make. I often wonder, was it really a dream, or did it really happen.

Chapter Twenty

Another two months passed and our life continued in the same vein. My brothers and sisters attended school regularly and I kept myself busy cleaning and preparing what food we were able to obtain. Circumstances had improved for everybody and our aunts, uncles and cousins did their best to make sure we did not go hungry.

Our clothing came from members of our extended family. These were "hand me downs"; clothing those cousins had grown out of and that were, of course, well worn! What we could have done with the money father had sent us! I often wondered whether our relatives regretted having spent the money as they did and if they felt guilty but I never dared ask anyone.

The boys were now completely absorbed in football, they were eating, sleeping and dreaming football. I was glad they were so preoccupied with their football they didn't have time to think about other things and it kept their minds and bodies active and healthy. My sisters, however, were sometimes upset and fretful, they missed their mother, particularly Antonietta, who was unable to grasp the concept of death and frequently asked when mum was coming back.

At these times my heart ached for them and I did my best to comfort them. Sometimes, when Antonietta was very upset I had to lie on the bed beside her, holding her tightly, till she fell asleep. Pina understood the situation better and, remembering our early days in Italy, she followed me everywhere, holding tightly to my hand. A letter arrived from Rome saying that children, who had come from North Africa, were to be repatriated. This was the most exciting news, just what we had been waiting for.

There were lots of official instructions we didn't understand, and which, frankly, did not interest us. We were interested only in the list of names of the children, living in the area, who were to be returned home. The children's names listed under the town heading included my name and that of my sister, Pina but the names of Antonietta, Emanuele and Marcello were nowhere to be seen.

Uncle Rocco contacted Rome but nobody was able to help him. He wrote several letters without success. After two or three weeks I was very concerned, I was determined that we were not going to be split up again. Either all five of us returned to Tripoli or nobody did. Uncle Rocco remembered my stance regarding the coffin transfer and realised that I meant what I said.

He, therefore, decided that he would take us to Rome to prove to the officials there that we really were a family of five and all five had to be repatriated. We were excited about the prospect of our trip to Rome. We had never been to the capital city and this time we would be travelling in comfort through Italy, not in the manner we experienced when travelling from the North of Italy to Sicily.

My excitement was tinged with sorrow, regret and apprehension, we were leaving mother behind. I had been aware that the time would come when we had to leave her behind and return to our father in Tripoli but I had become so accustomed to her reassuring presence which was reinforced when I visited her grave.

During one of these moments of sadness and doubt I distinctly felt a hand on my shoulder, I turned to see who was there - there was no one! I knew then everything was all right; my mother had made it clear she would be with us wherever we were!

The time came for us to leave Sicily, we packed our pathetic little bundles and I took a last long look at "our" cellar. The memories of the last two years brought tears to my eyes, we had lost most of our childhood from the time we left our parents in Tripoli. I knew how I had suffered and wondered how it would affect the rest of my life. We thanked all those who had helped us said our "goodbyes" and made our way to the Rail Station.

As we anticipated this journey was much different, the train was comfortable and travelled very fast. We were still able to take in the scenery, which was lovely. Despite all our heartaches suffered in this country, it was beautiful. I vowed there and then that I would return to Italy from Tripoli in the future. Such a journey, however, would be made on my terms and it would be for pleasure. I also vowed I would return to visit my mother's grave in Sicily.

Chapter Twenty-One

We arrived in Rome, it was a very large city and everyone seemed to be in a hurry. Rushing around, sometimes pushing and shoving each other to get wherever they were going faster. Leaving the station we had to make our way on foot to the department that would deal with our repatriation.

We were impressed by the beautiful buildings around us, some of which I recognised from the pictures I had seen in the history books we used in school. I could not take it all in, there was just too much to see. Our uncle was preoccupied, he had no idea where the department he wanted was situated in this very large city. He enquired of a policeman and we were directed to a building where I am sure it said War Ministry.

Uncle took us upstairs to one of the offices where he was able to see someone who held quite a high position. He told the story, time and time again but the official did not seem to believe him or was unable to understand. Uncle Rocco was becoming exasperated and angry. The official went off to consult with someone but two hours later we were still waiting.

We were finally informed that there was no trace of any papers in relation to the two boys and Antonietta. I was able to explain that Antonietta had not come to Italy with us but had come later with our mother. This might explain why they could not trace papers for her. It was pointed out that my brothers had come with my sister, Pina, and I and there should be, therefore, the same papers for them as us. More time passed and no one seemed to be doing anything or accepting responsibility.

In exasperation my uncle said he would leave the five of us there and someone would then have to take responsibility for us. Whether he would have carried out his threat or not we don't know but we were apprehensive and afraid. More time passed and our concern increased. A young woman then appeared and told us arrangements were being made for us to stay at a hotel for the night and the matter would be sorted out tomorrow. This, to us, was good news we were excited about the prospect of staying in a hotel, especially in Rome.

Uncle Rocco was not so pleased, he was complaining bitterly that he was losing money - he had his fishing boat and the crew could not sail without him. We had to travel by bus to the hotel, which was small and not very imposing. It was clean and comfortable and to us it was luxurious. The hotel had been notified that the Ministry would pay for our accommodation so the lady on the reception desk made quite a fuss of us.

She was trying to find out the details of our circumstances but uncle Rocco was very uncommunicative so she was left in the dark. I later heard her describe us to the porter as "refugees". Uncle was anxious to see us settled in; he was out of his depth, having never before had to look after five children on his own.

We were accommodated in two rooms, each had a double bed but these were large and soft. There was plenty of room for the three girls in one bed and the two boys shared the bed in the other room. Uncle was given a single room. He was hopeful things would be sorted out the following day and he would be able to return to Sicily.

Despite his brusque manner uncle Rocco was a caring man. He had paid for mother's visit to the specialist in Palermo, and was with us here trying to ensure our return to Tripoli as a family. He even paid for our journey to Rome, I will always be grateful to him.

After our tiring journey, we all slept very well, luxuriating in the warm soft beds. I awoke refreshed and woke the girls up. There was a bathroom attached to each of the rooms and I filled the bath with hot water. I saw Pina into the bath then woke my brothers; I filled their bath too and told them to enjoy this unexpected treat. Returning to our room I prepared Antonietta and made sure she had a warm bath too.

As they dressed I allowed myself to soak in the wonderfully warm water, this was luxury beyond my dreams. When we were all dressed I regretted that our clothing was so shabby but this could not be helped. Uncle called us for breakfast and we went downstairs. The tables in the dining room were covered with sparkling white cloths, cutlery was laid ready for use and there were napkins and cups and saucers. We were astonished; we had never seen anything like this.

We sat round the table and made short work of the crisp fresh bread and sweet milky coffee provided. We thanked the hotel staff and boarded the bus to take us back to the Ministry. Arriving quite early, we were greeted by the same young woman from the previous day. She was very polite, but told us regretfully we would again have to wait. Her assurances that everything would be sorted out gave us encouragement and we were much happier.

Our good night's sleep and our wonderful bath had gone a long way to making us feel physically much better and putting us in a better frame of mind. After some two hours, the young woman returned carrying a bundle of papers. She was smiling. "All the necessary forms have been processed," she told us, "You will be transported from Rome to Naples where you will be taken by boat to Tripoli." We could hardly believe our ears; we jumped for joy and hugged one another. Uncle Rocco managed a smile with his sigh of relief.

"You will have to hurry," said the young woman, "Your transport will be leaving Rome shortly." We were astounded - all this waiting and now we had to rush to get ourselves to Naples. A man in a blue uniform appeared enquiring where the other passengers were, he quickly took charge and escorted us to the rear of the building where a coach was waiting. There were some other twenty children already seated and the driver lost no time in setting off.

There were no checks made to ensure that everyone who should be there were in fact on the coach. I was just glad that all five of us were together and at last on our way back to our home. Despite all the excitement, I dozed off and was surprised to be awakened by Marcello telling me we had arrived.

The harbour at Naples was a bustle of activity, there seemed to be people everywhere and an awful lot of machinery. Despite the seeming confusion, we were shepherded on to our boat very quickly. The officials in charge were very efficient and much less austere than those we remembered loading us on to the boat in Tripoli so many years ago. Uncle Rocco, who had, of course, accompanied us to Naples, handed us over to the officials. We tried to thank him for all he had done but he quickly said goodbye and departed.

I was taken aback by the speed of his departure he did not even make sure we were boarding the right boat. I felt rejected but at the same time thought that our uncle was overcome with all that had taken place. The important thing was we were on board the ship that was about to return us home. Asking if our father would be informed of our return we were assured he would be informed we were returning on a specific ship from Naples.

We were allocated beds but the boys had to go with all the other boys while we girls were allocated beds with the girls. There were several hundred children on board which reminded me of our journey from Tripoli but that was the only resemblance. This was a passenger ship, there were proper cabins and beds and those in charge were not at all like those we had encountered then.

After settling the girls I went to make sure the boys were all right. Emanuele could not contain his excitement at being aboard this large ship. He did not remember his journey from Tripoli seven years previously. I warned Marcello that he must not let Emanuele out of his sight. While not unpleasant, the journey seemed to take along time but we made the best of it and, on the whole quite enjoyed it. We slept well were able to take showers and the food, though plain and simple, was, to us, very good.

Chapter Twenty-Two

The journey gave me time to reflect on the time we had spent away from our home. It had been seven years since we left Tripoli, my brothers and I were now in our teens, Pina was eleven and Antonietta seven years old. It was difficult for me to picture our father and I was sure the younger children would not remember him or our grandparents.

I wondered how our family would reconstitute? The five of us had bonded very tightly when it was necessary for us to look after each other in order to survive. Our life together, in "our" cellar was something special. We had shared traumatic experiences that children should not be exposed to and if we had not supported one another would not have survived. We solved our problems together and we had become a close-knit family unit.

All these thoughts were racing around in my head, now that we were finally on our way. We did not now have to worry about returning home this was a reality. However, contemplating our future taxed my mind. What would my father's attitude be towards us, would he appreciate that Emanuele, Pina and Antonietta did not perhaps remember him?

Would he see this as rejection, or would he understand. Would he appreciate that we had become an independent entity or would he consider this defiance and rebellion on our part? All these questions went unanswered I was confused and somewhat apprehensive.

Other factors intruded on these thoughts, why had my father not accompanied my mother when she came to find us. Why had he allowed her to shoulder this burden on her own? There had been no communication from him for several years, the war finished two years previously, why had he not come to us? Although I knew the answers to most of these questions they still nagged me and created doubts in my mind.

Standing on the deck of the ship I was acutely aware that this was the journey my mother desperately wanted to make. I felt unhappy and was aware of the sadness in my heart especially at this time when I should have been filled with joy and gladness. As I wanted to be alone with my thoughts, I had sought out a secluded part of the deck.

Thus it was a young sailor came upon me unexpectedly and, in a clumsy sort of way, he made amorous advances. I think he was trying to kiss me. I quickly made my escape, but was secretly flattered as this was the first time anything of this nature had happened to me.

As we neared the port of Tripoli we could see the Palm trees standing out against the white buildings of the Lungomare (the esplanade). It was a beautiful day, the sun was shining and there was not a cloud in the sky. This was our home it was a wonderful sight and it was an exhilarating experience for us.

We finally sailed into the harbour the engines stopped and the ship tied up alongside the quay. We were all on deck, trying desperately to recognise our father in the crowd of parents on the quayside below. Every child on board had the same idea, everyone was milling around trying to reach the most advantageous position. On the dock the adults were trying to spot their children among the sea of faces and when a parent recognised a child and called them by name there was crying and shouting on both sides.

The noise and excitement was intense, there was considerable confusion but happiness too as children left the ship to a joyful reunion with their parents. Those remaining were able to move nearer the rails to look anxiously for their families. We were right against the rail but were still unable to see anyone we recognised as our father.

Eventually we were given permission to disembark and we walked from the gangplank to stand together rather forlornly, nobody rushed up to us offering a warm embrace! As people left there was less confusion, we saw a man and a woman approaching. A faint recollection of the photograph of father came to mind but this man looked older and the woman at his side was a complete stranger.

The man spoke, calling us by our names, he was our father. He greeted us by name and kissed each of us in turn. Introducing the woman as Josephine he said she was his housekeeper. He turned to me saying, "I know what you must have gone through, looking after your mother and the other children, you deserve a rest, I will take over responsibility."

I had waited a long time to hear my father say these words but something inside me made me feel unsure. It was like asking a mother to hand her children over to a complete stranger, my maternal instinct in relation to my siblings had grown so strong. My sisters lined up on either side of me each holding a hand tightly. Why should we feel like this?

After all this was our father whom we had been longing to see for so many years. He had even engaged a housekeeper to look after our physical comfort, so we should be feeling very grateful. Josephine however, did not instil confidence in us, despite her words of welcome. Her tone of voice was such that her words seemed to lack warmth.

We climbed aboard a horse drawn taxi and headed for home where our grandparents awaited us. I searched for landmarks, desperately trying to recognise the area but I was surprised when father said, "Here's the house, we've arrived." A little old lady was standing at the door and behind her an old man was also approaching the door.

These were the grandparents we could not remember. Grandmother was sweet, kind and gentle, she kept kissing and hugging us she was so pleased to see us. Our grandfather was less demonstrative but conveyed his pleasure at our safe return. We all sat down around the table and enjoyed a meal of Pasta followed by cheese, and fruit picked from our own garden. It was the finest fruit I've ever tasted. As we ate father told us we could all now relax as he was here to look after us and our day to day needs would be dealt with by Josephine. Josephine bustled around smiling; she made a few inconsequential remarks but did not appear very interested in what father was saying. I watched her with a growing feeling of unease; she reminded me of the "teachers" who were supposed to look after us when we first went to Italy. Perhaps I was just too suspicious after all we had been through. Our father knew it would not be possible for him, even with grandmother's help, to work and look after us properly so he had engaged Josephine to ensure our domestic well being. I would no longer have to worry about whether my sisters and brothers had clean clothes etc. Life was going to be much easier for me. It was sad that we could not have our dear mother with us but we were all together as a family once more. I felt a little uneasy, too, that my father did not ask about my mother's illness and eventual death but concluded that he wanted to spare our feelings.

Chapter Twenty-Three

After our meal we unpacked our few belongings. Our accommodation was very limited, we three girls had to share a bedroom with grandmother and the two boys shared a room with grandfather. This left father with a bedroom to himself and when I asked grandmother about this she told me that Josephine shared with father! When I discovered the sleeping arrangements, a sick feeling engulfed me.

I felt our mother had been betrayed. This woman, fifteen years my father's junior, was not just a housekeeper. From that moment I disliked her intensely and knew she and I were going to be incompatible. I kept these thoughts to myself, deciding I must assess the situation further. I helped my sisters and brothers settle down and grandmother tried to assure us that everything was going to be fine. She later confided in me that she disliked Josephine intensely.

Father was now working as Fire Chief for the Shell Oil Company and this entailed night shift working. Often, after father had left for work in the evening, Josephine would dress up and go out, not returning till the early hours of the morning. This, coupled with her indolence so far as the domestic running of the house was concerned, made us angry and unhappy.

I was particularly frustrated, as my life had changed very little. It is true that I did not have to worry about food, there was plenty to eat and our clothes were provided. However, I still had to make sure that we had clean clothing and I often had to rise early to prepare breakfast, as Josephine was still fast asleep after her late return to the house. We were naturally curious as to where she went. All of us assumed that our father was aware of these late excursions so nobody dared to bring up the subject.

My domestic responsibilities had not changed very much and my relationship with my father was not progressing, as it should have done. My brothers and sisters still depended on me as Josephine did not encourage any close relationship and did very little in the way of caring for us. My grandparents were too old and even they were, to a great extent, dependent.

It was difficult for us to transfer our dependency to father, as he did not seem to understand our needs. He was too taken up with Josephine, she seemed to make him feel younger and he had become accustomed to being a free agent without the encumbrance of five children. He did not appear to appreciate what we had been through and seemed almost to resent us being there.

He never mentioned mother, Josephine had taken her place in his eyes. This I could not accept and, indeed, I often wondered just how hard my father had tried to contact us or send money when we so desperately needed it. My dream of a reunited family had not materialised. Although the five of us still related well and there was the added support of our grandparents the family atmosphere was missing.

Our father seemed only interested in his work and his "Josephine"; it was almost like living in the house of a stranger. For several months our lives continued in the same vein, but gradually Josephine transferred the household chores to me. Her demands increased and I began to feel like a drudge. It had been different when there was no other adult to be responsible for us and I had to take charge but this was not the same, it did not seem right.

More and more Josephine went out in the evening when father had gone to work returning even later in the morning and staying in bed longer. One evening, Emanuele and I decided we would follow Josephine when she went out. We planned it very carefully as we knew she must not see us.

She walked to Tripoli town centre, she had taken care to dress herself in an outfit that was tight fitting and quite revealing, she was heavily made up. First she went into an apartment block just off the main street, we dare not follow to find out which apartment she visited but had to wait till she reappeared.

After some twenty minutes she came out of the building retraced her steps to the main street, walked further down and entered a bar. She sat at a table and ordered a drink. After she had been sitting for about ten minutes, two American soldiers entered the bar and joined her at the table. They appeared to know her very well, they laughed and joked together and the soldiers bought her drinks.

A short time later time one of the soldiers leaned across the table and, placing his arm very intimately round her shoulders, said something which made her laugh and she nodded her head. The two rose from the table and made their way through a door to the rear of the premises. About fifteen minutes later they reappeared and rejoined the other soldier at the table.

Emanuele and I looked at one another, we were very naïve and this behaviour puzzled us. Then the other soldier rose and he, too, walked to the door at the rear with Josephine. Again, after some ten or fifteen minutes they returned to the table. When the two soldiers left the bar Josephine sat alone at the table once more.

She sat there, sipping a drink, for some twenty minutes when she was joined by an American Air Force Sergeant. He, likewise, seemed to know her very well. The sergeant ordered drinks and they talked and laughed together for some minutes longer. Then he became more familiar, he put his arm around Josephine's waist pulled her towards him and pressed an amorous kiss on her lips, she responded immediately and several kisses followed.

Innocent as we were, my brother and I realised that Josephine was not as she made out to be. This was nothing new to her and she obviously had more than one such liaison with these foreign servicemen. We had seen enough; we were shocked and hurried back home. On the way we said very little, we were too embarrassed. We did, however, agree that our father must be told.

I tried to tell my father that Josephine was going out at night when he was at work but his response was that he knew about this. He said, "She has a very good friend who is ill, this lady was good to Josephine when she was very young and she feels she must help her now." I could not believe how gullible my father was, he appeared to trust her implicitly.

I decided that if it were not possible for me to convince him he would have to find out for himself. I hated Josephine for her deception. More and more it was left to me to deal with the domestic chores. Quite often she would lie on the bed next to my father when he was sleeping during the day. He would awake to find her by his side and he was flattered. We knew, however, that she was catching up on her sleep and I was angry that I had to do the work.

The situation became more upsetting to me, I talked to grandmother about it and she said, "Santina, the woman is wicked, she has sold most of your mother's belongings but your father will do nothing, he is afraid of losing her." I tried to talk to Josephine about the situation, I wanted her to know that we were aware of what she was doing and that we felt it was very wrong.

I suggested that my father should know if she did not intend to change her life style. Each time I broached the subject she laughed, saying, "Your father will not believe anything you tell him, he believes I am visiting my sick friend." I knew she was right, my father was besotted with her and did not want to upset her for fear of losing her. I had to find a way of resolving this problem for the sake of my father and for all the family.

I formulated a plan, if all the doors were bolted next time Josephine went out at night she would be unable to let herself in with the key. I talked to my brothers about it. My older brother, Marcello, would not become involved, he maintained that it was none of our business what she did or where she went. So long as father was happy with the situation he felt that was fine by him.

I could not make him understand that she was deceiving everybody and that father was being used by this woman for her own ends. I told him I could not let it continue. Emanuele was enthusiastic about the plan; he shared my dislike of Josephine. I did not involve my two young sisters.

Accordingly, the next evening my father went off to work and Josephine made up and dressed herself in clothing, which left little to the imagination. We were ready. As soon as she left the house Emanuele and I made sure all the doors were firmly bolted on the inside, so it was impossible for anyone to let themselves in with a key. I decided to sleep in father's bedroom, which was at the front of the house, so that I would hear Josephine on her return.

What a luxury it was to stretch in a large double bed. To think of my father sharing this bed with a woman like Josephine made me seethe with anger. Especially when I thought of the cramped conditions my sisters and I had to endure. I could not remember ever having slept in such a large bed on my own before and it was not long before I was fast asleep.

I awoke with a start and looked at the clock beside the bed. It was 3 a.m. and the sound that had wakened me was that of a key grating in the lock of the front door. It was Josephine who had returned and now found she could not unlock the door. She tried several times then went to the back of the house where she had no more success.

She knocked quietly on the back door, to which, of course, nobody responded. She then went back to the front door where she knocked again several times. This knocking was not very loud at all, she did not want to arouse the neighbours Again there was no response and after a few minutes everything went quiet.

I waited for another half hour then I rose from the bed and went quietly to the front door. There was no sound, I felt a little guilty knowing how cold it could be at this time of the morning but hardened my resolve knowing that I was doing this for the good of the family. Emanuele was asleep but I woke him and we slid the bolts back silently on both of the doors.

I went back to bed where, despite the trembling of my body, nature prevailed and I was soon fast asleep again. I again woke with a start; it was my father unlocking the door. Suddenly he realised there was a bundle on the veranda. I jumped out of father's bed, quickly rearranged the bedding so it appeared not to have been slept in. I ran as fast as my legs would carry me to my own bedroom

Father had gone to the bundle and, realising it was Josephine, was obviously stunned. "What are you doing here?" he asked. There was disbelief in his voice, he was obviously puzzled. Josephine answered, "I couldn't get in, there is something wrong with the locks."

As she spoke she rose from the veranda, Father's voice, which till now had been little more than a whisper, rose suddenly, "What are you dressed like that for?" he said, "You look like a tart!" Josephine, in turn, became angry, "How dare you call me a tart," she shouted, "I've had to spend the night huddled on this cold veranda and all you can do is criticise my clothes. After sleeping in them all night what do you expect?"

Father turned again to the door which opened with no effort, "There's nothing wrong with the lock on this door I don't know what you are up to lady", he said, "but I don't like it!" He pushed Josephine inside and then he saw me standing there. I pretended I had been wakened by the commotion and asked what had happened.

Father glared at me suspiciously, "You didn't have anything to do with this did you?" he growled. I acted the innocent saying, "What do you mean?" Josephine glared at me. I believe she now saw me in a new light. She had not thought me capable of something like this until father had sown the seeds. Her expression was of utter loathing, "It was you, you scheming little devil," she shouted. "You must have bolted the doors, that's why I couldn't get them open, then you unbolted the doors before your father came home, you bitch!"

Before I could open my mouth my father lunged towards me. He rained blows on my head and when I raised my arms to protect myself he continued to strike me with a force that made me reel backwards and almost fall over. Such was the violence of his attack that I screamed out loud. All this noise roused the whole household, even my grandfather, who was hard of hearing.

Everyone ran into the room and father shouted, "Get back to your rooms, this has nothing to do with you". Marcello realised what was happening and immediately came to my side and wrapped his arms around me protectively. "What are you doing, no matter what she has done she doesn't deserve such a beating!" Father was taken aback, for a moment I thought he was going to strike my brother as well. Josephine stood there with a gloating smile. "What are you smiling about?" He roared. "Pack your bags, woman," he shouted, "I never want to see your face again!"

Josephine paled visibly; she had never seen my father in such a rage before. She rushed to the bedroom, hurriedly packed her suitcase, and wasted no time in leaving the house. It was obvious she was afraid of my father's anger being turned on her. Fortunately for all of us we never saw Josephine again.

My father, I felt, had vented his anger on me because he knew I had uncovered Josephine's deceit and made him aware of it. He was still angry with me for he had lost his sleeping partner and this obviously meant a great deal to him. I think, too, he felt some guilt for the vicious way he had attacked me. For whatever reason, my father hardly looked me in the face after this.

The only time he spoke to me was to give orders, "Do this, do that". I found it difficult to manage the household. Although grandmother tried to help she was old and frail, often she could not even get out of bed. My younger sisters tried to help but when my father saw this he would stop them. I was not going to be forgiven for what I had done.

The days were long. Both my brothers worked now but their employment was outside the city so it was necessary for them to be transported. The transport collected them at 5 a.m. as work started at 6 a.m. Because of the intense heat it was necessary for them to start early before it became too hot. Thus it was I had to rise at 4.30 a.m. to prepare their packed lunches and ensure they had breakfast before they left for work.

My father vetoed any suggestion that my brothers should assist in these preparations. It was made perfectly clear that my role was to housekeep for my father and my brothers and there was no way I would receive any assistance. After my father and brothers had left for work, I busied myself collecting all the clothes etc ready for washing. I then had to waken my sisters, prepare them for school and see them off. It was then I had to clean the house, do all the washing and ironing and prepare the midday meal.

Anything that did not please my father resulted in a quite violent slap on the head. Although I was glad Josephine had gone, there were times when I regretted being responsible for her leaving. I sometimes felt that my father had deserved her and I should have let him continue in his own sweet world of fantasy.

However, I knew that it had been in the interests of the whole family that she should leave before she decided to leave herself. When she felt it was time to leave, I was sure that it would have been when she had got her hands on all of my father's money and the family would have suffered even more.

I suppose I was now thinking of myself and how I was confined to the house. I was not allowed to meet friends or join in anything that other teenagers were enjoying. Whenever I asked if I could go out with other girls my father replied, "You have better things to do than go off gallivanting." I would conceal my hurt and disappointment, shed my tears in private when nobody was around and generally suffer in silence. I would often think of my mother and ask for help and guidance. "Dear mother," I would say, "How long can I go on like this, I sometimes feel I would be better dead, I don't feel that my life is my own, please, please help me". When I talked to my mother like this, I always felt better. It was as if she were there to reassure me.

Chapter Twenty-Four

Every hour of the day was spent attending to the needs of others. I felt a prisoner in my own home. I had to find a way of changing things. In desperation I decided I must gain some freedom. I would have to sneak out during the afternoon when my father was asleep. I had to take the chance that he might wake up and find I was not in the house.

Although I only visited a girl friend, Adele, who lived around the corner these escapes from my humdrum existence kept me from going mad. On these visits I encountered Ernesto, Adele's older brother, I was immediately attracted to him. I had never felt this way before about a boy. Ernesto appeared to be attracted to me also; he kept on asking me to meet him.

He said we should get to know one another better. My answer, as always, had to be the same, "My father does not allow me to go out". Ernesto would look at me in disbelief, I 'm sure he felt I was making excuses because I did not want to see him. If only he knew. I was desperate for a relationship with someone because my life was so empty.

I started taking an interest in my appearance. I showered and washed my hair every day, I wore my best clothing hoping that, by chance, I would meet Ernesto. From my back garden I could see the front of his house. Often I would stare at his house, hoping for a glimpse of him. Several times he, too, looked for me and when we saw one another we communicated in our own sign language. This intrigue made my life more tolerable.

On one of these visits to Adele, she passed a note to me from her brother. I could not wait to read it. I rushed home, locking myself in the toilet in order to read the note. With trembling fingers I unfolded the piece of paper and read, "Dear Santina, Please meet me this evening in front of the church, I must talk to you, I think I am falling in love with you, Ernesto". I read the note over and over again; my heart was beating faster and faster. I had to find a way to meet Ernesto; I desperately wanted to see him. How on earth was I going to do it, how could I get away? I tried to persuade my grandmother to make an excuse for me to be out of the house I told her why I wanted to go; I knew she was a romantic at heart. However, she was afraid that my father would be very angry if he ever found out. If he suspected I was meeting with a boy he would go berserk and would blame her for conspiring with me. She advised me not to go.

There was no alternative, I had to take the risk of going out without permission, I was determined I was going to see Ernesto and if I was found out I would have to suffer the consequences. My father was now on day shift and would not return home till much later in the evening. I hoped to be back in the house before he returned. Getting myself ready, I checked my appearance in the mirror; I wanted to look my best.

Marcello knocked on the door and came into the bedroom. He asked me where I was going and I told him I had some shopping to do. He looked at me suspiciously, "You never go shopping," he said. "I have run out of some things I need for the evening meal, I'll have to get them so I can cook the meal before father returns from work." I knew he didn't believe me and, as I bent to fix my shoes, the note from Ernesto fell from the pocket of my blouse.

Marcello picked it up, read it and said, "You lied to me, and this explains everything." With that he left the room, I knew he would tell my father the whole story. Why did nothing work out for me? I stood in the bedroom staring at the window. Should I go to meet Ernesto now anyway, accepting the fact that I was already in trouble?

I did not have to think too long about this, however, as my father returned from work early and was immediately appraised of the situation by Marcello. Father started shouting at me, "What do you think you are playing at, I have forbidden you to have anything to do with boys. It is obvious you are not to be trusted; from now on you will not step out of this house unless you are accompanied by one of your brothers. Do you understand?"

I was shaking with both fear and anger at my father's outburst. I nodded my head in acquiescence, tears rolled down my cheeks. "Mother, mother, mother," I kept saying under my breath. My father then said, "Get yourself into the kitchen and cook our evening meal."

It was several days later when I saw Ernesto at the front of his house. He was gesticulating in our sign language. He made me understand that he was disappointed that I had not kept our tryst. It was impossible for me to explain without being able to talk to him. I would dearly have liked to tell him to ask Marcello why it had not been possible for me to meet him.

At that moment I decided that it would be impossible for me to meet anyone my father disapproved of. I might just as well accept my situation. So long as I did exactly as my father dictated things ran smoothly in the home. I felt that it was not worth making all the family unhappy by worsening the tensions between my father and myself.

I was now sixteen years old and I had not experienced much happiness in my life I was desperate to find some way of improving my future. Perhaps it would be better if I could find a job. Going out to work would, at least, allow me contact with people other than my immediate family. I knew it was going to be difficult to persuade my father but perhaps the contribution I could make to family finances would provide an element of persuasion.

Being careful not to do or say anything to upset him, my relationship with father became a little easier. He thought he had, at last, gained my submission to his will. Communication between us, however, was virtually non-existent. It was two months since the incident with Ernesto; I avoided looking towards his house so I did not see him. On the couple of occasions he called at the house on the pretence of seeing Marcello, I went into the bedroom. He could not understand why I was avoiding him.

I did not understand why Marcello had never said anything to him about the incident; perhaps he was feeling guilty and ashamed. After all we had been through together he betrayed me like this without even talking things through. Ernesto asked Adele to pass a message to me but I told her I no longer wished to be involved. I knew it would be impossible to have a relationship with Ernesto without Marcello finding out. To go through the same trauma again was not an attractive prospect at all.

One day, out shopping, accompanied by my father, of course, I saw job advertisements. I decided this was my opportunity to ask if I could go to work. His reaction was not unexpected, "You dare to talk about going out to work, your place is in the home cooking and cleaning, looking after your brothers and sisters, your grandmother can't do it."

I was devastated, I walked quickly ahead of him; I needed to get home as soon as I could, tears were choking me. Going straight to the bedroom and finding grandmother was not there, I looked in her cabinet to see what medication she had. I was looking for tablets to end this miserable existence. No longer could I continue living like a prisoner. Life was just not worth living.

I was now sobbing aloud and, hearing this, grandmother came into the room. "Whatever's the matter," she asked. "I no longer want to live like this." I replied. "What do you mean?" she gasped, "I thought things were better now." "No Grandma," I sobbed, "I've had enough, I'm sorry I must leave my family but my father has driven me to this. Don't try to stop me, please, my mind is made up."

Grandmother noticed her cabinet drawer half open. "What have you done, where are my tablets? She asked anxiously "I don/t know," I lied. She began shaking me, "Please, please, Santina," she pleaded, "Don't do this to me, I feel guilty enough already that I can't help, I know how unhappy you are but this is not the way to resolve things." She was sobbing with me and, in desperation she called my father. "Get a doctor," she cried, "Santina's taken an overdose." Father ran for the doctor who, fortunately, lived nearby. Within minutes they returned and the doctor gave me salt and water, which made me violently sick, I felt terrible. The doctor tried to question me but I refused to talk to him.

For several days I was upset and refused to talk to anyone. My father tried to talk to me but I refused to converse with him. Grandmother had obviously talked to him about my desperation. In his heart he must have known it was his intolerable attitude that was causing all the trouble.

After two weeks, of my refusal to speak to my father, when we were seated at the table for our evening meal, my father said to me, "You can look for a job but I will still expect you to attend to all the chores as usual." This came completely "out of the blue" and despite the fact this meant I would still have to rise at four o'clock in the morning to prepare packed lunches for him and my brothers, it was music to my ears.

I was sure he felt I would not want to work outside the home and still look after the family but I was determined that my life had to change. Thus it was, I agreed to his terms and said I would look for work right away. I applied for a couple of jobs but I was unsuccessful, as I had no experience.

A friend I had known from school, Natalina, called to see me one day and she said she'd ask her mother if I could help out at the Laundry. This was her mother's business and Natalina went there in the afternoon. She told me her mother needed assistance sewing on buttons and making minor repairs to the clothing presented for laundering. I was thrilled by this idea, I didn't really care what I did so long as I went out of the house. I was certainly well experienced in sewing and mending. The fact that Natalina would be there too meant that we'd see each other every day.

Natalina's mother was happy with the idea; she knew it would be company for her daughter as well as a help to herself. It was agreed that I would work on a part time basis and I began to make plans in order to manage all the housework as well. I did not want to give my father any opportunity to complain that I was neglecting any of my household chores.

I commenced work and, although my father insisted on escorting me to and from the laundry, life became more tolerable and certainly a lot more interesting. I found it exciting meeting people. There was a constant stream of British soldiers coming and going, the laundry had a reputation for providing a good service. The soldiers were, of course, mainly young men and several of them would try to involve Natalina and myself in conversation.

They were far from home, in a foreign country, and, naturally they were eager for female company. As we didn't speak English and they didn't speak Italian this made it very difficult, and it led to many funny instances. Some of the soldiers could be uncouth but Natalina's mother was very protective towards us. She was quite a large lady and did not stand for any nonsense.

All of this was very new to me and, despite my feelings of trepidation, it boosted my confidence and I began to feel that I was worth something. Although Natalina was younger than me she had become accustomed to the soldiers and would flirt with them quite openly. Of course, she was assured of her mother's protection and the soldiers were quite respectful in their conduct. As I have said those who were not got short shrift. I became more assured and would sometimes flirt with the soldiers too but I was very guarded.

If my father had any inkling of this I would no longer be allowed to work there and my life would be even harder than before. Several soldiers asked me to go out with them but my answer was always the same, "My father does not allow me to go out." Occasionally my father would turn up at the laundry during the day, he would make some excuse for being there but I knew he was checking up on me.

Chapter Twenty-Five

After I'd been working at the laundry for some months, I noticed how a Scottish soldier kept on looking at me. The first time he called at the laundry, I remembered, was one very hot afternoon when Natalina was sitting on the step, as it was so uncomfortably hot inside. This soldier was working on the telephone lines on poles round the barrack walls. He saw Natalina and came over to the laundry on the excuse that he wanted to collect his laundry. I later discovered he had no laundry with us)

He was "chatting up" Natalina and she came inside to ask her mother about the laundry. The soldier followed her in and we saw each other for the first time. Although he did not say anything to me at that time, he did then start bringing his laundry on a regular basis. He began to have conversations with me, which was often quite amusing, as we did not really understand one another. As time progressed he, several times, asked me to go out with him.

Unlike the other soldiers he was very persistent, he would not accept that it was not possible for me to go out with him. He bought an English/Italian dictionary and tried hard to communicate, he insisted he had fallen in love with me. It was very difficult for me to make him understand my situation.

He came from a background where these restrictions did not exist. I found him attractive but knew if I suggested to my father that I wanted to go out with a British soldier my days working at the laundry would be over. This situation continued for several weeks and the soldier, Jim, kept asking me to go out.

One day he told me that he knew where I lived and that he intended calling on Saturday to ask my father's permission to marry me. I thought he was crazy, "You can't come to my house, my father will throw you out. If he thinks that I've had anything to do with a soldier he will stop me coming to work altogether" Jim was not convinced, he said if I didn't ask my father's permission to come out with him, he'd take a chance and call to see my father himself. It was difficult to make him understand how obsessed my father was. Jim kept saying it was our culture. I told him that these were rules laid down by my father; I had to abide by them and so would he. Jim would have none of it, he was adamant that if I didn't approach my father that he would. By this time we were sure of our feelings for each other and, despite my fear of the consequences, I really did want to establish our relationship.

I dreaded the idea of Jim turning up on our doorstep unannounced and the reaction this would provoke in my father. I had nightmares about it. I tried several times to broach the subject with my father but it was never the right time - or I was just too scared. I decided to confide in my grandmother, she sat there listening attentively to every word I had to say. Although she smiled from time to time I was not sure what she was thinking.

When I finished telling her how I had met this wonderful man, how he made me feel very special and how persistent he was in wanting to share his life with me, grandmother clasped her hands in front of her chest and said, "How romantic, this is something I never had, at least not with your grandfather." I asked her what she meant.

My grandmother explained that her marriage to my grandfather had been arranged between the families and, while she was very fond of my grandfather she had never really loved him. She went on. "Shortly after I was married I had an encounter you think only happens in films I passed this man in the street, he stopped and looked at me for a very long time. I could feel his gaze, I looked back, he was tall, blonde and very handsome. I felt myself smiling at him; I believe it was love at first sight.

Certainly I had never felt anything like this before. Seeing the smile as encouragement he approached and walked beside me. He spoke and his voice sent shivers down my spine. His Italian was perfect but he spoke with a foreign accent. He attempted to strike up a conversation but although I felt I wanted to throw my arms around him and never let him go, I was shaking with fear. If anyone saw us my life would not be worth living.

Reluctantly, I walked on, I didn't dare look back, I knew if I looked at him again my resolve would disappear despite the inevitable consequences. "My grandmother seemed to be in a world of her own, her eyes held a sparkle I had never seen before. She told me she had never forgotten this man, he became her fantasy lover and when my grandfather made love to her she imagined it was the tall blonde stranger whom she never knew but who had captured her heart.

She then continued, "Santina, don't let anyone convince you to marry anyone you don't love. You should fight to marry this man if you truly love him and, be assured I will help you all I can." This was the encouragement I needed, I decided to tell my father and devil the consequences.

It took me a couple of days to summon enough courage to speak. I chose a moment when I thought my father was in a good mood. "I want to tell you something," I said, "Promise to listen and not start shouting, please hear me out." My father looked at me suspiciously, "You're not going to ask to go out with your friends again, are you?" He asked. "No, listen, please, I have fallen in love, I want you to meet this young man, he wants to ask you if he can marry me."

"I have never heard such rubbish in my life, he said. "I decide if and when you marry and whom you are going to marry. I've already had an offer of marriage for you; I was going to tell you in the next few weeks. He's a bit older than you but he's a doctor and will be able to look after you well."

I could not believe what I was hearing and my grandmother's words came back to me, they gave me the courage to retort, "I'll never, never marry someone you have picked for me, someone I have never even met. Times have changed, you cannot and will not force me into an arranged marriage." I ran out of the room, my heart pounding. I went to grandmother in tears, she was shaking, too but told me to stand up for what I wanted.

Later as the family sat round the table for lunch I tried to act normally. My father suddenly turned to Marcello and said, "Listen to what your sister has to say, she's in love and wants to get married." His tone was mocking and he smiled in a very sarcastic manner. I was stung to retaliate, "Yes, I am," I said, "This is something you would not understand, being in love, I doubt if you could ever love anyone." I immediately knew I had gone too far.

My father said nothing but his expression told me everything. He rose and came towards me, he struck me several times around the head and shoulders, they were painful blows and I started to cry. Then my father spoke, "You will never know how much I loved your mother, she was everything to me, how dare you say I could never love anyone." He turned on his heel, went to his room and stayed there for the rest of the day.

Perhaps he felt guilty, despite his love for our mother he had a strange way of showing his love for us. He may even have felt that it was our fault he had lost his love in such a tragic manner, without even being able to say goodbye. Marcello tried to talk to me, questioning me, who was this person, how had I met him? When I told him about Jim he was horrified, a British soldier, a foreigner.

He told me father would never allow such a marriage. I begged my brother to intercede on my behalf. To try to persuade him to meet Jim, at least, before dismissing him out of hand. After all, I pointed out it was I who would have to live with him if we married. Marcello was finally persuaded and agreed that he would meet Jim and that he would try talking to my father, I hoped that, at least, he would listen to him

Two days later, Marcello told me he was prepared to meet this young man but he had not been able to change father's mind. My father did not want to know anything about this soldier. So far as he was concerned the arranged marriage was going ahead. Even Marcello was unable to change his mind about this. So deeply entrenched was his attitude that I could see no hope at all.

Despite my despair and despondence I was determined to carry on. I was encouraged in my resolve by my grandmother who was a tower of strength. I'm sure she had a lot of influence over Marcello as well. I arranged for Jim to come to the house on the next Saturday afternoon to meet Marcello. The atmosphere in the house was tense.

This was not the way I wanted Jim to meet my family but he insisted on coming assuring me he understood the situation. I was not so sure that he fully understood the position as we had difficulty in communicating in two languages with neither of us being competent in both. I was scared, Jim didn't know what a Sicilian father could really be like.

The day for Jim's visit arrived, I rushed around cleaning and dusting over and over again. I made sure all were wearing their best clothes; I wanted to make a good impression. Grandmother gave me money to purchase cakes and a bottle of Vermouth. She certainly supported me in making my young man welcome. I was not sure about Marcello's feelings. He was very quiet, I was sure he was going to make it clear that the family did not approve of this liaison.

As three o'clock approached, I became more anxious. It had been agreed that Jim would be at my home for three. I kept going out on the porch looking frantically down the road. My heart was beating very fast, my head felt as though it would explode. I kept praying to my mother, "Please help me, I know you understand, please, please make my father understand too. I cannot marry a man he's selected for me, someone I have never met, I must marry the man I love."

I saw Jim coming up the street; he looked so handsome, tall and blonde. I waved to him and went to meet him at the gate. He took my hand and I hoped my father would not see this, as I was fearful of his reaction. However I led him into the house and managed to get my hand out of his before we actually stepped into the room where my brother, Marcello was waiting.

Everyone was naturally curious but grandmother ushered them all, except Marcello, out of the room. My father came out of his bedroom, said nothing to Jim but indicated to Marcello that they should sit at the table. Marcello was fluent in English so was able to act as interpreter. My father sat down, lit a cigarette and eyed Jim up and down. He then indicated that I, too, should leave the room and, through Marcello began interrogating Jim. After almost two hours of questions and answers, my father got up from the table and went into his bedroom.

The visit was, apparently over, Marcello stood up, he shook Jim's hand and asked him to leave. I did not know what had transpired, I didn't know whether they'd told Jim never to see me again or what had been said. Going to the gate with Jim, he tried to make me understand what had been said. He was able to convey to me that he'd virtually been told to go away and get the necessary permissions from his parents and his Commanding Officer before he could ever see me again.

If permission were given from those sources, my family would be prepared to discuss the situation further. Marcello had acted not only as interpreter but also as intermediary but I think he probably told father that this would put Jim off and that they would be unlikely to see him again. He had also, however, given Jim hope that having gained the necessary permission my father's agreement would be forthcoming.

Little did he know how my father's mind worked. Jim did not seem too upset about the outcome and tried to assure me that everything would be all right. He smiled and strode off whistling. I was not so convinced as he and dreaded the next few weeks. On the following Monday, Jim came into the back room in the laundry. He embraced and kissed me passionately. I was overwhelmed. I knew he still wanted to marry me but was horrified that he had kissed me. He managed to make me understand that he had already written to his parents who already knew about me, but he had now told them he wanted to marry me. As soon as he had their approval, he would approach his Commanding Officer to obtain the necessary official permission to marry a "Foreign National".

I was in turmoil, what had he done? His intentions were honourable but he had spoiled everything by kissing me. I cried all night, when my grandmother saw my face in the morning, she said I would have to be patient and trust Jim that he would persevere. "You don't understand," I sobbed. "I think I'm pregnant." "My God, Santina," she gasped, "What have you done, how could you let this happen?" "I don't know," I replied, "It just happened, my father will kill me now for sure."

Overcoming the initial shock, grandmother asked, "When did this happen, you haven't been alone with this young man, you have not been out with him. How could you possibly be pregnant?" "It was at the laundry," I said, "In the room at the back we were alone there, yesterday." "I wish it had never happened, now but it was so sudden, he held me and kissed me." My grandmother asked, "Was that it?" I nodded.

She looked at me strangely, there was the hint of a smile on her lips, and I thought how could she possibly smile at a time like this. "Are you sure that's all that happened?" she asked, "What more could happen?" I retorted. Then grandmother did smile and putting her arm around me said, "My dear, dear child, it takes more than a kiss to get you pregnant." I did not understand, I knew nothing about the facts of life. Nobody had ever explained or even mentioned these things.

My mother had never had the opportunity and now any talk about sex in our house was taboo. I felt a great sense of relief, I had been upset and had felt angry with Jim, as I thought he had taken advantage of me. The thought of being pregnant had filled me with a great fear. I was fearful that my father would kill me or at least disown me and throw me out of the house. He would certainly have forbidden me to have anything further to do with my family and that alone would have broken my heart.

My first kiss should have been a wonderful experience; instead it had brought me fear and unhappiness because of my ignorance. That same night my grandmother told me the essential facts about sexual relations that made me even more determined that I could never marry a man I did not love. I knew I had to see Jim and try to make sense of our future.

It was almost three weeks later that he came to the laundry; he did not look at all happy. I had a great sense of foreboding. Jim told me his parents, although counselling him against marrying a foreigner, had said they would not stand in our way if we felt this was right for us, he had, therefore, obtained their consent. He had also talked with his Commanding Officer who had said something similar, the glamour of a foreign girl, etc. etc.

The outcome was that the Officer had decided to send Jim out of Tripoli to one of the Desert Posts for six months. The reasoning behind this was, if after six months Jim still felt the same way permission would be given for us to marry. I had mixed feelings about this, I knew that I would miss him but felt that it would be better for us both to be separated so that we could be sure of our true feelings.

It worried me that perhaps my home situation was influencing me too much and precipitating me into a relationship. I knew my feelings were genuine but I just wanted to be sure and this six months separation would certainly prove to both of us whether it was true love we felt for each other. Jim was not happy with the idea but knew there was nothing he could do about it.

Chapter Twenty-Six

I felt I had to widen my knowledge. Working at the laundry was all very well but my world revolved around the laundry and home. It was time for me to look for another job where I would meet more people and broaden my horizons. An uncle told me of a position in a Stationery and Photography shop in the centre of the city. This sounded just the sort of job I was looking for so I applied and was successful. My father was not too keen but was persuaded by my grandmother that it would be better for me to be employed in the city and to contribute even more to the family finances.

When I left the laundry I asked Natalina and her mother not to let anyone know where I had gone to work. I don't really know why I did perhaps I felt that if Jim really did love me he would find me again. The job in the shop was a real challenge for me, lots of British and American servicemen visited the shop and I had to try and serve them. I began to learn more English and was quite proud of myself.

These young soldiers often flirted with me and several of them asked me to go out with them. My answer always had to be the same, "My father does not allow me to go out with men, particularly soldiers." Their attentions, however, were flattering and I began to think, perhaps I was not so unattractive after all. Certainly I was growing in confidence and, although I often thought about Jim, I was certain that it was not a bad thing at all that we had been separated for a period.

I was very happy in my employment; despite all the chores I had to attend to in the home, which I dared not shirk. I knew my father needed only the slightest excuse to stop me from going out to work. My two younger sisters helped me so far as was possible. They were very interested in my love life. Every day they asked when I would see Jim.

Both my bothers were fully employed and were enjoying their work. Marcello, particularly, enjoyed what he was doing as he was interpreting for the British Military Police and his command of English was very good indeed. They both worked well and did not cause any problems for me.

Life at home was better and I was able to buy myself some of the things I needed as a young woman. My father seemed to feel that my relationship with Jim was a thing of the past. However, I still felt a longing to see him again and wondered if he really thought of me. Work continued to be enjoyable and the soldiers still kept coming in the shop.

Two were persistently flirting with me and asking me to go out. One was an American Air Force Sergeant and the other was an Irish Guardsman. It was amazing how they both kept coming to the shop but they never ever visited on the same day. I enjoyed their attention but did not know how long they would keep coming, as I had to refuse all their invitations to go out.

Life was better, although I still longed to see Jim, as it was now more than six months since we had been together. I saw Natalina. She told me that recently Jim had appeared several times at the Laundry and kept on asking where I was working as he so desperately wanted to see me.

I asked Natalina if Jim had the necessary permission that my father and Marcello had told him they required. Unfortunately, Natalina did not know and I was so concerned that he had not obtained permission that I made her promise not to tell him where I was working. I knew he would not dare to call at the house if he did not have the necessary permissions.

One Monday morning shortly after my conversation with Natalina a British soldier walked into the shop, I was facing away from the counter and he asked for a pen. His voice was familiar, I spun round and there was Jim standing before me. He stared at me in amazement, "So this is where you are," he said, "I've been looking all over for you, I've been asking Natalina almost every day where you were but she would not tell me."

He looked jubilant that he had found me at last, "Santina, I now have permission from my parents and from my Commanding Officer to get married, I must come and see your father." I stood there, speechless; I did not believe what I was hearing. I was so glad to see him; I'd missed him so much and knew for certain that I loved him. I told Jim I would arrange for him to come to my home but warned him that nothing had changed. My father and brother thought they would never see him again so he would have to be patient and be prepared for a less than warm welcome.

Dear granny was once more my confidante. "What am I to do? " I asked her, "I know that my father will place every obstacle he can in the way, how am I to convince him that this is the man I want to marry?" Granny was her usual calm self but gave me some devastating news. She told me that my father had made arrangements for me to meet the man he expected me to marry. He had, she said promised this man that he could marry me on my eighteenth birthday.

I could not believe what I was hearing. How dare my father make arrangements for me to marry someone I had not even met. This really convinced me that my father believed he was not going to be bothered by Jim again. I knew I had a battle to fight but, undaunted, I managed to make arrangements through my brother, Marcello, for Jim to meet with my father.

I had to find out how Marcello felt about the whole thing, he had persuaded my father to meet with Jim again but I knew how loyal he was to father. However, I knew also that my brother was a man of honour. We had gone through a lot when we were on our own in Italy but I could not judge how much he was prepared to fight on my behalf.

As soon as Marcello returned from work I engaged him, "Marcello, you know that Jim has obtained permission as you asked him to do and he now wants us to be married, I also want to marry him, please, you must keep your promise and talk to father, I can't marry someone I have never even met." Marcello asked if I had approached father, I told him I had only talked to grandmother who was prepared to intercede on my behalf.

Marcello agreed that Jim and I had done all that was asked of us, "I think it is only fair that you are given a chance to see if you are suited to one another. Particularly as you are still determined that you wish to marry and spend the rest of your lives together." Dear, dear, Marcello, at least I could rely on him.

Marcello tried to discuss the situation with my father without much success. He was adamant that his arrangements for me to marry the man he had chosen would stand. He said to Marcello, "That decision is final, I don't want to hear anymore from you or your grandmother." This response angered even Marcello, normally he would not argue with father but he felt that at least he should be prepared to discuss the situation and not just assume that everyone would go along with his plans.

Jim came to the shop the next day. I told him my father was still against our marriage and seemed determined that I should marry this person with whom he'd made arrangements without my knowledge. Jim was sad and upset, he put his arms around me and said "We are not going to let anybody stop us from getting married, we love one another and that is the most important thing."

I knew that even if in the end I forced the situation, my father would not pay for a wedding, we would have to be content with a very small celebration. I conveyed this to Jim who said, "I'm saving all my pay we will manage somehow." It was reassuring to know that he was considering the practicalities of our future as well.

Jim explained to me that it had not been easy to obtain the permission of his parents either. Initially they had refused permission, saying he was too young, he was in a foreign country and they did not want him to marry a foreigner. He had been devastated by this attitude, he wrote to them again saying, "If you do not give your permission I will end my Army career in North Africa and when I am old enough to marry without permission I will marry the girl I love and probably make my home here where she has her family."

Two weeks later both parents reluctantly gave their permission. Jim also explained that it had not been easy obtaining permission from his Commanding Officer. They too, considered him too young and felt that it was possibly only an infatuation. It was for this reason they insisted we be separated for six months. If after the six months we still felt the same and his parents had given their permission then he would be allowed to marry. Despite all that had been done we were still having difficulties with my father.

Jim came to our home on the following Sunday, father deliberately stayed away and Marcello was polite but cool. My grandmother tried to make him feel at ease but the language barrier made it difficult. She did not even speak much Italian but her conversation was conducted in a broad Sicilian dialect that Jim could not understand at all. The visit was not what one would call a great success. My grandmother encouraged me to fight my corner.

She told me her own marriage had been arranged and, while grandfather was a good man, they had nothing in common. He worked very hard, from the early hours of the morning till the late hours of the night He was a quiet industrious man who was not much fun to be with. Granny had conceived twenty four times but only seven children survived. When miscarriages occurred grandfather was no comfort he took everything in his stride in a very matter of fact way and expected everyone else to do likewise. He was not an emotional person and certainly lacked passion.

My grandmother told me how she had felt very lonely throughout her married life. Although, initially, they had been quite wealthy the drought conditions in Sicily caused them to lose crop after crop and eventually they had to sell most of their property. Their four daughters had to be provided with a suitable dowry according to the established custom - no dowry no wedding. My grandparents ended up living with their eldest son, my father.

Being a proud man, grandfather found it difficult to accept the fact that he had to depend on his son for all his needs. Being left with no means of supporting themselves they were completely dependent but grandfather would never ask for anything and, basically, became a recluse within the family.

I had always felt sorry for him but he was never prepared to talk about his situation. I now understood better what he was feeling and I was fascinated listening to my grandmother describing her life. This was the first time she had dared to discuss her relationship with grandfather. My situation was making her determined that I should not accept my father's decision and that she was prepared to support me in my fight to spend my life with the man I loved.

Me at the age of 16

Chapter Twenty-Seven

Despite my father's insistence that things would be as he dictated, my determination was such that my family began to rally round me. Grandmother, particularly, was vociferous in her condemnation of father's stance and Marcello, too, was surprisingly supportive. In the end, the resistance to my father's plans was too much even for him. Eventually he saw it was fruitless to hold out against the whole family.

He did not, however, give in gracefully. One evening he pointed at me saying, "You have been nothing but trouble to this family, now go your own way and be damned!" This meant I had won but not in the manner I'd desired. I wished my father to listen to reason and to see my point of view, to move on from the out dated customs of Sicily. Instead he remained entrenched, convinced he was right, reluctantly admitting defeat and, no doubt, blaming me for enlisting the family support.

Although my fight was over there was a bitter taste and my father's words had hurt me terribly. Jim became a regular visitor, whenever his duties allowed he would call in the evening and at weekends. Father always left the room when Jim arrived but gave strict instructions that we were never to be left alone. Even when we went out together we were always "chaperoned". My grandmother arranged our chaperone; she dare not go against my father's wishes in this respect.

I began to feel that perhaps my father had not capitulated so easily and was making things as difficult as possible hoping we would become so disillusioned and frustrated that eventually, we would give up all hope of being married. He could not have been more wrong. We became even more determined to be together as a proper couple and started making plans for our wedding.

Jim was the only one who could save as my father took all my earnings and gave me no money at all. He also indicated that he certainly would not attend the wedding. I was saddened and upset as, despite his actions, he was my father and I would have much preferred to have his blessing and for him to join in our celebration and happiness. I asked my grandmother to try to persuade him to relent but he was adamant that the only wedding he would attend would be to the man he had chosen for me.

I wanted to be married in a proper white Wedding Gown but where was I going to get the money to buy such a dress. A friend who had married two years previously, offered to lend me her wedding dress, she was my size and I was so pleased and excited. Another friend and neighbour offered a dress suitable for Natalina to wear as she had agreed to be my bridesmaid. A Maltese family, with whom we had become friendly through a Scottish civilian friend of Jim's, offered their eight-year-old daughter's services as bride's attendant and said they would supply her dress etc.

Things were beginning to look much better and I was determined that nothing would stop us having a proper wedding. We started looking for somewhere to live, we possessed nothing but our clothing but we were determined to manage. The date for the wedding was arranged, 27th January, 1951. We would marry in the Church of the Christian Brothers, this was a Catholic Church used by the English speaking community in Tripoli.

The Church was run by a group of Monks from Malta and the Military Padres conducted services there. We were to be married by Captain

Kelleher, a Catholic Army Padre. Jim had arranged a Reception at the NAAFI Social Club in the Castle by the main harbour in the city. Everything was going according to plan; I could hardly believe it was all happening. Invitations were sent.

Of necessity it was not going to be a lavish affair and so only a few relatives and close friends were coming. I was very apprehensive. How would I explain my father's absence and who would "give me away"? Although I tried several times, my father refused to discuss the issue. In a last desperate attempt I tried to persuade him to change his mind but this ended in us having a terrible row.

I was so enraged by his attitude and upset by the hurtful things he said, I decided I could not stay under the same roof any longer. When Jim arrived I was sobbing with hurt and anger. I grabbed his arm and ran outside. I told him I was leaving home, I didn't know where I was going but I was not staying a moment longer. Poor Jim, was confused, he didn't know how to respond, he didn't want to be the reason for me leaving my family before we were married.

I kept on walking very fast, away from the house. I was sobbing and kept saying, "I can't stay here one more day." Jim kept asking me where I was going to go but I couldn't give him an answer as I just didn't know. We walked aimlessly for some two hours but couldn't come up with a solution. Although we had found an apartment to rent this was not available to us till the day before the actual wedding.

Jim suggested we approach some of his married friends who lived with their wives and families but I didn't feel I could cope with that As it grew dark I decided to visit an Aunt who lived not too far away from my home. This was my father's younger brother's wife. She agreed I could stay and said she would get uncle Pino to talk to my father the following day. Knowing I was now safe, for the night at least, Jim returned to his barracks.

The next day, my brother, Marcello, was concerned by my absence. Nobody knew where I was and my father only expressed his anger that I had disappeared. Marcello ended up having a row with father and went out looking for me. He called at uncle Pino's house and was relieved to find me there. He put his arms around me and said, "I appreciate how you feel, but, please, Santina come back home. I will do what I can to help with your marriage, you are both obviously determined to be together."

I agreed to return home with him but made it clear that there was now only a couple of weeks to go to my wedding day and I was determined that nobody was going to stop me from marrying. Now, too, I had the support of my older brother, despite my father's uncompromising attitude.

January 27th today is my wedding day. My father rose early, dressed, ate his breakfast and left. He said nothing to me but acted as if I didn't exist. I cried, this was supposed to be a very happy day for me. In my desperation I called to my mother, "How different things would be if only you were here." I felt her presence around me and took comfort from this I heard myself saying aloud. "Please stay beside me throughout this day, I am entering a life unknown to me, I don't know if I'm doing the right thing I need your strength to support me I promised you I would look after my brothers and sisters but knew that, eventually, I would have to leave them.

I cannot cope with father's attitude, he is just so unreasonable. Please mother give me a sign that you are here with me and approve." Suddenly, I felt calm and reassured, I was convinced my mother was beside me I wiped the tears and went to find my two younger sisters. I hugged them very tightly, kissed them several times and assured them that, although I was getting married, I would always be there for them.

I then sat alone reflecting on my past and wondering what the future had in store for me. I told myself to stop thinking of all the sad times, and to enjoy what should be the happiest day of my life. I was determined that I would enjoy it and that everything was going to be fine. I showered; my face was still red and swollen from all my crying. I wanted to shout and scream to release the tension in me.

I heard relatives arriving so composed myself and called for my sisters who then helped me to dress. My uncle Mario arrived with my aunt in their quite luxurious car. He was a rich, successful builder. Uncle Pino had previously said he would give me away but then decided he could not really go against his older brother's wishes. This did not concern Uncle

Mario, my father's brother-in-law who immediately said he would be happy to walk me down the aisle.

The bridesmaids arrived, they looked lovely. My borrowed dress fitted me perfectly and Jim had sent the bridal bouquet. Everything was in place and we set off for the church, the bridesmaids and I in my uncle's car. As we entered the church I saw Jim in his kilt, I thought he looked very handsome.

I walked down the aisle on my uncle's arm, my only regret that it was not my father's arm. As we reached the front, Jim smiled at me lovingly and he looked very proud. Suddenly it all seemed right and my life now had a meaning. Although the service was conducted in English and I did not fully understand what the priest was asking me to repeat, I put my trust in Jim that everything was in order.

So the ceremony proceeded in the time-honoured fashion regardless of the language used. This was the language of love and we were committing to each other, as we truly believed our future was together despite the differences in our race and culture. After the ceremony, we left the church to find two pipers waiting and they walked in front playing us to the car outside. This was Jim's Commanding Officer's car and driver.

We were driven to the Old Castle by the harbour where again the pipers played us up the steps into a lovely panelled room. The castle is an historic building part of which was being utilised as the NAAFI club for British servicemen. All my family, with the exception of my father, attended. All of Jim's friends and several of his officers also attended.

The room was full of baskets and bunches of flowers. The custom among Italians then was to give flowers rather than presents when one married. The manager of the club' who was a friend of Jim's had prepared a buffet lunch and provided a three tier wedding cake. I was astonished that Jim had been able to provide all this for us. At the end of the party the guests left wishing us every happiness and we were escorted to our apartment in the middle of town.

We settled down to our married life. We had only been married a couple of weeks but I was fretting that I had not become pregnant, in my innocence I expected to be with child immediately and thought there must be something wrong with me. After two months however, I was expecting our child, we were delighted. From the outset my pregnancy was not pleasant, I suffered badly with morning sickness.

I was very concerned about my sisters and brothers, feeling guilty at having left them. Pina, my younger sister, had been forced to shoulder the burden of my previous responsibilities in running the household. Poor girl, she really was too young at 14 years of age, particularly as our father's expectations were so high. Remembering my own teen years made me more upset for her.

Pina did visit our apartment but this was unknown to my father as he forbade the family to visit. After a few months Pina informed me that father had a new lady friend and it looked as if plans were being made for them to marry. I was not sure if this news was good or bad. I had not met the lady and knew nothing about her. My father still refused to have anything to do with me.

The only consolation was, if he married then hopefully, his wife would take over the running of the household and Pina would be able to live her own life. I tried to make peace with my father. I desperately wanted to remain an integral part of my family. He could not find it in his heart to forgive me for my defiance of his wishes. I had married someone he had not chosen for me.

By this time, Jim and I had started to visit the family home and, while father did not oppose this, he completely ignored us. The other members of the family were fine towards us and Jim was totally accepted by everyone else. My father, however, ignored him and acted as if he did not exist.

Our Wedding Day

Chapter Twenty-Eight

I continued to be adversely affected by my pregnancy, constantly being sick and whenever I was in a hot, humid atmosphere I felt faint. My need for my family was intensified by my illness. On one of my visits home I met my father's "intended". She was a very nice person, of a similar age to my father but she had never married. Employed as cook to a British Colonel and his family she seemed a very "homely" person and very brave to take on an "instant" family including our grandparents.

I really wanted it to work out this time; Luisa was entirely different to Josephine. An added bonus, for me, was that the British had employed her and she was very enthusiastic about them. Luisa and my father did marry but Jim and I were not invited to the wedding. It made me very sad but as time passed, I realised that the family appeared to be happy.

Luisa had taken control of the household and, while she too was dominated by father, she was also very efficient and able to look after the family very well. My sisters and my brothers seemed to like and respect her and she certainly "mothered" them. To know that they were now being looked after properly made me much happier and more contented in my own mind.

In due course I was admitted to the British Military Hospital and gave birth to a beautiful little girl whom we named Giovanna, in memory of my late mother. Things did not go as expected, however. After only 24 hours Giovanna was very ill. This being a military hospital it was not equipped for an emergency such as this and I feel, too, that the staff were not very experienced in dealing with babies.

Our lovely baby lived for only 48 hours; yet again our very dearest had been taken. What had I done to deserve so much unhappiness? I had lost an enormous amount of blood during the birth and I was kept in hospital. Jim went to my family to tell them the news. He was very upset and crying when he told them the drastic news. When he visited me in hospital later he told me my father had appeared upset and had been quite human towards him.

The loss of our daughter affected me drastically. I found myself feeling more and more depressed. Jim helped me through this, despite his deep feeling of loss too; he was more resilient than I was. Then came the devastating news that Jim's battalion was to move to Egypt. He managed to persuade his officers that he should not be sent immediately and was allowed to stay behind as part of the "rear detail".

Their function was to hand over the barracks and equipment to the regiment who arrived to replace them. This was only for a period of six weeks but it helped me overcome my depression. Eventually Jim had to leave for Egypt and I felt as though part of me had gone.

Fortunately, during the period before Jim left, we had moved in with my uncle Pino and his family. This meant I was much nearer my family home and was able to see my sisters and brothers on a regular basis. Of course, they were also able to visit me in my uncle's house.

Another blow came! We received the news that Jim's battalion would be returning to Britain. The troopship would call at Tripoli for only 48 hours to embark the families of the regiment. I wanted to be near my brothers and sisters, but my father was still unforgiving and this made me very unhappy. I decided to talk to Luisa and ask her to intercede with father on my behalf. I really wanted to patch up our difference before I left for Britain.

On my next visit home it was obvious Luisa had spoken with father, he did speak to me. He said how saddened he was when we lost our little girl. He would, he said, have been very proud to have his first granddaughter. I put my arms around him. I could not speak but my tears flowed freely.

I began to pack our belongings and, of course, came across the clothing we had bought for our baby. It was now five months since our tragic loss and I had visited our little Giovanna's grave almost every day. Seeing the clothes made my grief well up again. We would now be leaving her behind also. I asked my mother to take care of her little granddaughter whom we had named in her memory. With all the upset I had dealt with in my own family life, I had not given much thought as to how things would be in England. My mind now dwelt on this as I remembered that Jim's parents were also against our marriage. It occurred to me that life could possibly be as difficult over there as it had been here and that Jim's parents might be just as awkward as my father had been. As we were going to live with Jim's parents in England and he would, after his period of disembarkation leave, be in Scotland with his regiment I realised I would be facing a daunting prospect on my own.

Chapter Twenty-Nine

As the time grew closer for the troopship to dock at Tripoli, so my apprehension grew. The thought of boarding a ship in Tripoli harbour brought back memories of the last time this happened. When, as a child, I left for a three months holiday, which lasted seven years and became a nightmare. Then my return to Tripoli, to the father who had become a stranger and the subsequent unhappiness I endured.

What now lay in store for me? In a foreign land that I knew little about and where the language used was so difficult I could barely communicate. The ship duly arrived, the soldiers were given their 48 hours leave ashore, just two days for the married personnel to reunite with their wives and families, ensure everything was securely packed and, eventually, everybody safely aboard.

I said all my farewells; my heart was aching as I took leave of my sisters and brothers. I assured them I would keep in touch and that I would save hard in order to come and see them. The day of departure was another sad day in my life. Although embarking on a new life with the man I loved, I was leaving behind all of my family and friends, the life and culture I knew.

The ship was certainly no " liner" and I had to share a cabin with other wives and children. The husbands, of course, were in the troop dormitories. They even ate with the other soldiers while the wives and children ate separately. I was not enamoured of the traditional British fare served up to us.

We were able to spend time with our husbands on deck and I fired questions at Jim as to how life would be in England, especially with his parents. Our trip lasted eight days and this seems long enough to have all my questions answered but, unfortunately, the sea was not kind. Particularly when sailing through the Bay of Biscay, I was stricken with terrible seasickness.

This made the journey much less pleasant and my powers of concentration much decreased. Jim did, however, try to answer my questions and relieve my anxieties but there were many he could not. He did not know how his parents and his sisters would react or how they would respond to me but assured me that nobody would hurt me and he would be there to look after me.

The ship finally sailed into Liverpool after eight days at sea. It was raining heavily and, although the middle of the day, the dullness made it more like late evening. Not knowing what to expect I was struck by the absence of sunshine and the houses looked rather strange and drab to me. I felt vulnerable and almost wished the boat would sail out again and take me back to Tripoli.

We were able to leave the docks and go immediately by train to Jim's parents' home in Shropshire. He had two weeks disembarkation leave in which to settle me down with his family. Sitting in the train on our journey to Shrewsbury, I was still apprehensive but looking at the passing scenery I was struck by how green the countryside was.

The weather brightened a little as the rain stopped and although still lacking sunshine, this land seemed less dark and foreboding. Arriving at our destination, I was surprised by the welcome I received. Jim's parents were excellent; they seemed genuinely pleased to see me and tried desperately to make me feel at ease. They too, were upset and disappointed that they had lost a granddaughter.

I shall always be grateful to them for making things so much easier for me. My mother-in-law was particularly good she treated me like her own daughter. Living with Jim's parents was not too difficult, I was completely accepted as a member of the family. Even my sisters-in-law and their families accepted me and treated me as part of the family.

Often there was laughter when I was trying to explain things in broken English but they laughed with me not at me. They were all very patient and helpful. I soon learned to speak English very well, albeit with a marked Scottish accent as I was with my mother-in-law most of the time and she was a broad Scot.

After three months in England I was expecting a child again. Jim and I were thrilled and the whole family was pleased. Unfortunately I was unwell for most of my pregnancy and given the history of my first pregnancy, everyone was very concerned. However, the doctors were kind and helpful and the hospital staff excellent.

I gave birth on the 13th. May to another beautiful baby girl who was perfectly healthy. We were ecstatic and named our daughter Silvana. Jim was posted to a local military unit and we were allocated married quarters within the barracks. We were then able to live as a family unit but with the added advantage of the extended family being close by.

Our baby daughter brought us great happiness and Jim's family was as happy as we were. My mother-in-law was a tower of strength during this time replacing in many ways the mother I had lost at such an early age. Jim by this time had transferred to the Royal Army Pay Corps and was eventually posted to a unit in Worcestershire. Again, my in-laws were a tower of strength during his absence.

When we were allocated quarters in Worcestershire I joined Jim there with our young daughter Life was more difficult for me without the presence of Jim's family but I gradually began to make friends with other wives and families. I became pregnant again and this time I was less apprehensive having undergone a successful pregnancy and birth on the last occasion.

Unfortunately again my life was marred by the untimely death of Jim's mother through cancer. Her passing devastated us both. I loved her for the substitute mother she had become to me. So upset was I that my pregnancy was threatened again. However, I was cared for by my doctor and eventually admitted to hospital in Worcester where, on the 31st July I gave birth to our son, Daniel.

Once again we were blessed with a beautiful, healthy baby. This went a long way in compensating us for the loss of my mother-in-law. Bringing up children is expensive but we tried hard to save money to enable us to visit my family in Tripoli. My brothers and sisters were constantly in my thoughts; I still felt considerable guilt for having left them so far away. I was concerned for my sisters, knowing how set in his ways my father was.

Despite letters telling me that things were fine and how good to them Luisa was, I still had a feeling of unease. This was due to my own experiences and the manner in which my father had curtailed my whole life. Jim eventually left the army and we moved to "The Potteries", Stoke-on-Trent, where he was employed by a National voluntary organisation.

Our family was augmented once again on the 21ˢᵗ. February, when I gave birth to another beautiful, healthy baby girl, Julia. We felt our family was now complete and, apart from various domestic pets through the years, this was to be the case. In 1963, we eventually had enough money to make the trip to Libya. At that time airfares were expensive.

We could, however, obtain discounted fares within the "sterling area", so we could fly much more cheaply to Malta. This meant crossing the Mediterranean by boat to Tripoli from Valetta. As this was only an overnight trip we didn't mind at all. So, finally we made the journey to Tripoli but the boat trip once again brought back unhappy memories.

These were soon blotted out by the joy of seeing my family once again. My father had aged and looked ill. He was still smoking heavily which did not help. Luisa made us very welcome and she obviously had become a mother to my sisters and brothers who were now grown up, very confident and appeared to be very happy.

They had their own children, I had mine, we were able to manage our lives and I could at last shed my feelings of guilt for having left them. My father had certainly mellowed with age and I'm sure the influence of Luisa had lot to do with it. Jim and Luisa built up a particular "rapport" I think possibly because of her long association with British army personnel.

My father and Jim spent a lot of time together, mainly playing cards - Jim lost all the time. Our first trip to my family was a great success. Despite the fact that my children did not speak Italian and my nieces and nephews did not speak English, they managed to converse very well and were quite happy together.

My father with his new wife and my brothers and sisters

Chapter Twenty-Nine

It was another six years before we were able to visit Tripoli again, this time my father looked much, much older and quite ill. Not the same person, he didn't dominate the family any more. Luisa was the dominant partner now and the family certainly had respect for her. They recognized the contribution she had made in cementing the family at a very difficult time in their lives. Thanks mainly to her, they were, now, all very successful and had very good life styles.

On this occasion our three children, Silvana, Daniel and Julia were all looking forward to the trip. We were persuaded to take with us Silvana's school friend, Elizabeth. We had a lovely time and my brother Emanuele and his wife, Anna, decided they would take the opportunity to christen their youngest child while we were there.

It was arranged for the last Sunday of our stay and on Saturday Jim went to the main post office in Tripoli and telegraphed B.E.A. (British European Airways) in Malta confirming our intention to take up our seats on the return flight to England. On Sunday afternoon the whole family and their friends attended the Cathedral in the centre of Tripoli for the christening.

After the service everyone returned to Emanuele's apartment to celebrate. It was quite a party, friends and acquaintances were continually dropping in with good wishes and christening gifts. Thus it was very late in the evening and the children were all very tired. Anna, my sister-in - law, suggested that our three children and Elizabeth should stay at the apartment and we could collect them tomorrow.

This was agreed and they went off to bed quite happily. Jim and I returned, with the rest of the family to my sister Pina's villa where we were all staying. This was some five miles outside the city but we arrived back there around midnight.

The following morning Enzo, Pina's husband, left the villa to go to his business in the city. As he was about to enter his car, a Libyan Army soldier approached and informed him he was contravening the curfew. Fortunately Enzo spoke good Arabic and was able to understand what he was told. During the night, apparently, an army "coup" had taken place under the leadership of Colonel Gadaffi. They had overthrown the Royal Regime, taken over all strategic points in the country's cities and imposed a curfew.

Civilians were only allowed to leave their homes between the hours of 9 - 10.30 a.m. when shops would be open for the purchase of food and essentials only. All telephone lines were closed and it was impossible to communicate with other parts of the city, country or the world. All banks and other commercial enterprises had been closed and only military personnel were allowed to move around.

We were completely cut off from our children who were, of course, in the heart of the city several miles away. I was shocked and stunned particularly as the police station had been taken over by the army. The para-military police, who were loyal to the king Idris Senussi, had been disarmed and locked up in their own cells.

My sister's villa was virtually mid-way between the army barracks and the police station and all this had taken place shortly after we returned home the previous night and we had seen and heard nothing. Jim with the agreement and assistance of Enzo decided to try to get into the city to ascertain if the children were safe. They went to the barracks where a group of soldiers were gathered by the gate.

A young officer, who was obviously well educated and appeared to come from a good family background was sympathetic, saying he had no objection to them travelling into the city to ensure the safety of the children. Before he was able to write the authorisation, however, an older officer of a lesser rank then the younger appeared. This man was obviously an enthusiastic follower of Colonel Gadaffi.

He said no foreign nationals had been or would be harmed therefore there was no necessity for Jim and Enzo to travel into the city and no authority would be given. He told them, in no uncertain terms, to return to the house. After he left Enzo again appealed to the young officer who said there was nothing he could now do but if they were determined to enter the city, he would do nothing to stop them.

They decided to make the journey and set off in the car on the main road to Tripoli. Every mile or so they were stopped by armed soldiers, searched for weapons and the car searched. When Enzo explained the reason for the trip the soldiers invariably shrugged their shoulders and allowed them to pass. When they reached the outskirts of the city, however, a more determined soldier argued vociferously with Enzo and threatened them with his rifle.

He was insistent that nobody passed and they were forced to turn around. Enzo, being well acquainted with the geography of the city, decided to try a different route and turned down a side street. They had only gone a few hundred yards when an army sergeant brandishing a revolver, stepped into the street forcing them to stop. He, like the previous soldier, was adamant they could not enter the city.

When Enzo argued with him he became quite irate and made it quite clear that if they did not turn around immediately they would be arrested. It was futile for them to continue arguing so with heavy hearts they reluctantly about turned and made their journey back to the villa. The same procedures, as on the journey going, were encountered on the journey back. Most of the soldiers were not too interested, however, and allowed them to pass.

When they returned we were relieved to see them but even more anxious as to the circumstances in the city. Why was the army so insistent that no one should enter the city? After three days of total anxiety we were able to make contact by telephone with my brother in Tripoli. He assured us everything was fine although there had been gunfire and some muffled explosions. We were able to speak to the children and Julia sounded quite excited when she told us "They were shooting down here!" It was a relief to know they were all safe but anxieties remained.

Things were better and some businesses had reopened, the banks, however, remained closed, as Colonel Gadaffi had sequestrated all monies deposited there. When and how would we be able to return to England.

Our flight tickets had expired so where did we stand. Jim telephoned the local office of the BEA (British European Airways) when he was informed that it would be necessary for us to purchase further flight tickets. This made us very unhappy and extremely angry. We, obviously, did not have the money to purchase six air tickets from Tripoli to England.

As the banks were still closed, my family were unable to give us cash. They had to conserve what cash they had to buy food, fuel etc. Nobody knew when or if they would be able to get any money Enzo, my brother-in-law. then offered to pay by cheque. Initially this was acceptable to B.E.A. but then when they heard the cheque was drawn on a Libyan bank they said they could not accept it. We had not taken a cheque book with us and could not, therefore, offer them a cheque drawn on a British bank.

Although the airports were still closed we would have to have our tickets booked in order to take advantage of any flight out of the country. In the meantime travel restrictions were relaxed and we were able to enter the city and were reunited with the children. Our next problem, of course, was how would we be able to get out of the country.

The only avenue left open to us was the British Embassy so we went with all the children to the embassy for assistance. Despite the circumstances the officials were aloof and unhelpful. They told us there was nothing they could do for us and that my family would have to help us. This infuriated Jim and he turned to the children saying, "Make yourselves comfortable, we are in for a long stay."

The embassy official was taken aback and asked what he meant. Jim told him that here we were a British family with a child from another British family, stranded in a foreign country with no means of support and no possibility of returning to Britain. It was, therefore, the responsibility of the representatives of the British government to offer help and succour. As we were in such a predicament we would stay in the Embassy where they could care for us.

At this point, the official - we never did discover his actual title or role - scuttled off and returned some twenty minutes later. He then said the embassy would purchase our return tickets and make arrangements for us to fly out on the first plane to leave the country. However, our passports were to be impounded on our arrival in Britain.

They would be returned to us only when we had repaid the amount expended by the embassy. Thankful that we were now assured of a flight home we left the embassy with our passports very visibly endorsed in bright red ink as follows: This passport to be impounded on return to the United Kingdom."

It was a total of eight days before we were able to communicate with the outside world again and let everybody in Britain know that we were safe and well. Shortly after we were informed that a BOAC (British Overseas Airways Corporation) plane would be leaving Tripoli Airport in two days time and we were booked to fly out to Valletta. A connecting flight to London, Heathrow would take us back to Britain.

We were able to contact friends in London and arrange for them to meet us at the airport. Eventually the time arrived for us to leave. While we were relieved to be going we were also concerned for my family. They were staying in what was, to say the least, rather an unstable situation. When we arrived at the airport we were met by armed soldiers everywhere.

We were "herded"- there's no other word for it - into a large aircraft hangar which was serving as a customs shed. Again soldiers on duty not customs officials and they opened every case and every bag. The children had bought small ornate trinket boxes for their friends. These were inexpensive but gaudily painted in red and gold. The soldiers seemed very interested in these examining them minutely, apparently thinking they were gold. Despite our protestations they confiscated them - to the dismay of the children. At last on board the plane everyone eagerly awaited take off. The plane taxied out to the runway and everything was ready for take off. Then, suddenly, the pilot announced that the plane had been recalled. The plane returned to the apron and the door was opened. Two armed soldiers boarded the plane and escorted the Captain off. Everyone was amazed and apprehensive, what had gone wrong, why had the captain been arrested?

After some twenty minutes the captain returned to the plane the door closed and, once again, we taxied to the runway. Another two minutes and we were off down the runway. As the plane lifted from the ground a cheer went up from the passengers and everyone applauded.

We later learned the cause of our return from the take off point. Apparently the major in charge of the airport had gone off for a cup of coffee (or tea) when the plane was cleared to taxi to the runway. As it was the first plane to leave since the coup had taken place, the major felt he must give the order. The lieutenant who did give the order in his absence was anxious that there should be no further delay in the plane leaving but only managed to defeat his object.

The captain of the plane was berated by the major when it had nothing to do with him. He took his orders from the control tower and acted accordingly We were more than glad to be leaving all this behind but there was still the nagging doubt about the safety of my family.

Chapter Thirty

Back in England we settled down to our life's routine and Jim progressed well in his employment. However, it took two years before our passports were returned, we had to pay back every penny, despite a long running battle with the foreign office and the airline company.

This experience left me very disillusioned with Libya. Despite the fact that our dear daughter is buried there I doubted whether we would ever visit that country again. My brothers and sisters had expressed misgivings as to their future in a country governed by Gadaffi. They felt it could become extremely unstable.

They all had businesses, however, and were dedicated to making a success of them for their own families' sakes. Their predictions were to come true, not quite as they expected. An outbreak of cholera in 1970 caused panic in Libya. Gadaffi refused to make available the anti-cholera serum to the Italian population of the country.

The Italian government, therefore, despatched a ship to Tripoli with vaccine for the Italians living there. At the same time offering any Italian, who wished to leave the country, free passage back to Italy. All of my family returned to Italy and, although they had made contingency plans for just such an occasion, they had to leave behind all they had worked for over the years.

My father, now seventy, had spent most of his life in North Africa. It was difficult for him to adjust to a new life in Italy. There was, however, no choice, he and Luisa had to go with the family. I know how my family must have felt, I often think of our life when we had no worries living in Tripoli with my mother and father. If Mussolini had not decided to ally himself with Hitler possibly none of these things would have happened.

A short while after his return to Italy my father died. It happened suddenly and I was unable to attend the funeral but this was like the end of a chapter in my family history.

My family, like me, had to make a new life for themselves in Italy. Despite the fact that we are Italian we were born and brought up in Libya. We still look back on our life there with nostalgia. The Italians did a great deal to improve that country but were repaid in a very contemptible fashion.

When my sisters and brothers had managed to overcome the trials and tribulations they had endured during their traumatic childhood and were successfully bringing up their own children all this had to happen. Once again their lives were turned upside down. Arriving once again in Italy in the same desperate fashion as they had left so many years before.

However, the Italian Government were sympathetic and very supportive. In all of those families repatriated those who were capable of employment were found positions compatible with their skills in State controlled enterprises. My sister, Pina, was employed in the Education Department and my brother, Emanuele, in the Ministry of Defence.

My brother, Marcello, was already working for Alitalia Airlines and so was transferred to a post in Italy. Antonietta's husband was employed in the Department of Finance and she eventually opened her own shop selling perfume, cosmetics etc.

Despite these traumatic experience my brothers and sisters appear to have stabilized their lives and I am proud of their achievements. To say, however, that these experiences have not had an adverse effect on them would be to ignore all they have gone through.

From left Antonietta, my younger sister, Emanuele and Pinuccia

Marcello, who had married a local girl in Tripoli progressed with the airline and settled just outside Rome. Their family consists of two girls and a boy all now settled with their own families. Emanuele who also married a local girl in Tripoli settled in Verona. They also had three children, two boys and a girl who are now independent family units in their own right.

Antonietta married my eldest brother's best friend, Giovanni. Having settled in Grosseto they had three boys. Again all are now settled with their own families. My sister Pina was not so fortunate. Like me she found herself at odds with my father who controlled her completely. His peculiar, old-fashioned Sicilian ideas and jealousies made life intolerable for her as it had for me.

She met and fell in love with a very presentable young man living in the Italian community in Tripoli. Of course, father would have none of it. So far as he was concerned it would be his choice when she married. Eventually, in complete defiance, they "eloped". This, of course, created similar problems to those I had encountered. However, they were married and soon started a family. They, too, had three children, two girls and a boy. Enzo, Pina's spouse, turned out to be somewhat of a Lothario and didn't stay faithful.

He was quite successful in business and the family had quite a satisfactory life style and the children did not really know what was going on. However, when the family moved to Italy his "affairs" became less discreet and he finally left Pina and his family to set up home with her best friend. Pina was devastated, she had never stopped loving him and certainly didn't look for another man in her life.

Her children, although upset, still managed to make their way in life. The eldest daughter is now a practising gynaecologist, the second daughter a qualified accountant and her son a sports journalist. They, too, have their own family units and, despite all their problems still very much a united family. As for me, I am older and wiser; my three children are very well settled within their own families.

The five of us many years later, from left Pinuccia, me, Antonietta, Marcello and Emanuele

Although, Jim and I are not rich, we enjoy a comfortable life style, my brothers and sisters have been able to visit us in England and we visit them in Italy frequently. Looking back on my childhood makes me realize how my life has changed and makes me determined that my children and grandchildren will never have to suffer as I did.

My Family

Photograph of the Author

www.ingramcontent.com/pod-product-compliance
Lightning Source LLC
Chambersburg PA
CBHW072115090426

42739CB00012B/2976